W9-CKI-261

Bloom's
GUIDES

Nathaniel Hawthorne's
The Scarlet Letter
New Edition

The Adventures of
  Huckleberry Finn
All the Pretty Horses
Animal Farm
The Autobiography of Malcolm X
The Awakening
The Bell Jar
Beloved
Beowulf
Black Boy
The Bluest Eye
Brave New World
The Canterbury Tales
Catch-22
The Catcher in the Rye
The Chosen
The Crucible
Cry, the Beloved Country
Death of a Salesman
Fahrenheit 451
A Farewell to Arms
Frankenstein
The Glass Menagerie
The Grapes of Wrath
Great Expectations
The Great Gatsby
Hamlet
The Handmaid's Tale
Heart of Darkness
The House on Mango Street
I Know Why the Caged Bird Sings
The Iliad
Invisible Man
Jane Eyre

The Joy Luck Club
The Kite Runner
Lord of the Flies
Macbeth
Maggie: A Girl of the Streets
The Member of the Wedding
The Metamorphosis
Native Son
Night
1984
The Odyssey
Oedipus Rex
Of Mice and Men
One Hundred Years of Solitude
Pride and Prejudice
Ragtime
A Raisin in the Sun
The Red Badge of Courage
Romeo and Juliet
The Scarlet Letter
A Separate Peace
Slaughterhouse-Five
Snow Falling on Cedars
The Stranger
A Streetcar Named Desire
The Sun Also Rises
A Tale of Two Cities
Their Eyes Were Watching God
The Things They Carried
To Kill a Mockingbird
Uncle Tom's Cabin
The Waste Land
Wuthering Heights

Bloom's

GUIDES

Nathaniel Hawthorne's
The Scarlet Letter
New Edition

Edited & with an Introduction
by Harold Bloom

BLOOM'S
LITERARY CRITICISM
An imprint of Infobase Publishing

Bloom's Guides: The Scarlet Letter—New Edition
Copyright © 2011 by Infobase Publishing
Introduction © 2011 by Harold Bloom

All rights reserved. No part of this book may be reproduced or utilized in any form or by any means, electronic or mechanical, including photocopying, recording, or by any information storage or retrieval systems, without permission in writing from the publisher. For information contact:

Bloom's Literary Criticism
An imprint of Infobase Publishing
132 West 31st Street
New York NY 10001

Library of Congress Cataloging-in-Publication Data
Nathaniel Hawthorne's The scarlet letter / edited and with an introduction by Harold Bloom. — New ed.
    p. cm. — (Bloom's guides)
    Includes bibliographical references and index.
    ISBN 978-1-60413-874-0 (hardcover)
    1. Hawthorne, Nathaniel, 1804–1864. Scarlet letter. 2. Adultery in literature. 3. Mothers and daughters in literature. 4. Puritans in literature. I. Bloom, Harold.
    PS1868.N39 2010
    813'.3—dc22
                                        2010024814

Bloom's Literary Criticism books are available at special discounts when purchased in bulk quantities for businesses, associations, institutions, or sales promotions. Please call our Special Sales Department in New York at (212) 967–8800 or (800) 322–8755.

You can find Bloom's Literary Criticism on the World Wide Web at
http://www.chelseahouse.com

Contributing editor: Portia Williams Weiskel
Composition by IBT Global, Troy NY
Cover printed by IBT Global, Troy NY
Book printed and bound by IBT Global, Troy NY
Date printed: October 2010
Printed in the United States of America

10 9 8 7 6 5 4 3 2 1

This book is printed on acid-free paper.

All links and Web addresses were checked and verified to be correct at the time of publication. Because of the dynamic nature of the Web, some addresses and links may have changed since publication and may no longer be valid.

Contents

 Introduction

The Western authorities on a nearly universal malady, sexual jealousy, are Shakespeare, Hawthorne, Freud, and Proust. *The Scarlet Letter*, one of the double handful of great American novels, is in some of its aspects untouched by the madness of jealousy, despite its pervasive theme of adultery. Only when Roger Chillingworth is the focus does Hawthorne's prose-romance take on the dissonances that recall Shakespeare's *Othello* and *The Winter's Tale* and that prophesy Freud's and Proust's analyses of jealous obsessiveness. Chillingworth is both a devil and an avenging angel, at once sadist and masochist, not only ambiguous in his own nature but extraordinarily ambivalent toward the Reverend Mr. Dimmesdale, his timid and equivocal usurper. Dimmesdale and Chillingworth are each other's victims, and yet each needs the other in order to go on living. The reader is likely to note that Chillingworth frequently seems more a portrait of Satan than of a seventeenth-century scholar-physician. In some ways the cuckolded husband of Hester Prynne is as occult a figure as Pearl—the faery-child of Hester and Dimmesdale—or Mistress Hibbins the witch. Much of what we think of as human psychology seems as irrelevant to Chillingworth as it does to Pearl and Mistress Hibbins. And yet the psychology of sexual jealousy is very relevant to Chillingworth: It helps illuminate the strangeness of his conduct, toward Dimmesdale in particular. The Shakespearean version of sexual jealousy—essentially inherited by all subsequent authors—is transmuted by Milton's Satan before it reaches Chillingworth. Something of the aura of Satan playing Peeping Tom as he spies upon Adam and Eve still lingers as Chillingworth contemplates Hester and Dimmesdale. But the archetype remains Shakespeare's Iago, conniving the destruction of Othello and Desdemona in order to enhance his own sense of self, or what Milton's Satan called his "sense of injured merit."

Sexual jealousy as a sense of injured merit may, in the last analysis, be the fear that there will not be enough space or enough time for oneself. In Chillingworth's instance, the extended interval that he seeks might be interpreted as the sadist's desire to prolong his satisfaction at his victim's torments, yet that would be inadequate to the complexity of Hawthorne's art. When Chillingworth desperately attempts to prevent Dimmesdale from pronouncing his revelation of guilt, we hear a multitude of motives mingling together:

> "Madman, hold! What is your purpose?" whispered he. "Wave back that woman! Cast off this child! All shall be well! Do not blacken your fame, and perish in dishonor! I can yet save you! Would you bring infamy on your sacred profession?"

We may doubt Chillingworth's concern for the good name of the clergy, but he certainly does have a considerable psychic investment both in the survival and in the reputation of Dimmesdale. For artistic reasons that have to do with preserving the romance element in *The Scarlet Letter*, Hawthorne does not allow himself, or us, an acute psychological analysis of Chillingworth (or of Pearl or Mistress Hibbins). If you do the devil's work, then you become the devil, and so we have the oddity that Iago and Chillingworth become considerably more diabolic than Milton's Satan ever manages to become, despite his titanic efforts. Chillingworth quite forgets he is a man and becomes an incarnate jealousy instead. His pride in keeping Dimmesdale alive is augmented by the clergyman's public image of holiness, while Chillingworth's deepest pleasure resides in the conviction that Dimmesdale ultimately will share in the physician's spiritual damnation, linked for eternity by their roles in Hester's tragic story.

Dimmesdale, caught between Hester and Chillingworth, has neither the blessed strength of Hester's balked capacity for life nor the infernal strength of Chillingworth's impotent hatred for life. The minister's character and personality, despite his acute sensibility, render him too weak to be tragic. When we think of *The Scarlet Letter* as a portrait of human character in dramatic conflict with itself, we are compelled to center on Hester, whose power of endurance is almost frightening in its sustained intensity. Dimmesdale is so pallid in comparison that we wonder how he ever provoked an extraordinary passion in Hester, who is so much superior to him in her capacity for an authentic life. Subtle as Hawthorne is throughout the novel, he is pragmatically sinuous in finding a multitude of ways to persuade us of Hester's sexual power. When he speculates that, but for Pearl, Hester would have been a second Ann Hutchinson, a major religious rebel against seventeenth-century American Puritanism, he associates his heroine with a violent energy, "the flesh and blood of action," that can only be sexual. Then *The Scarlet Letter* would have been a realistic tragedy, since Hester in full rebellion would have become a prefeminist martyr, immolated by the righteous men of Puritan Boston.

Readers now, as we have entered a new millennium, may be tempted to undervalue the courage and physical stamina that Hester manifests in maintaining her seven-year defiance of her entire society: its religion, morality, and sense of election by God and by divinely decreed history. Hawthorne never violates her dignity, her self-reliance, her loyalty to the unworthy Dimmesdale. At least a century ahead of her own time, Hester would be fierce enough to die for her sense of self were it not, as we have seen, for her maternal obligations. Yet she is too large and passionate a being to have any sense of injured merit; within limits she bears her outcast status as the cost of her confirmation as a natural woman, and her consciousness of her own "sin" is highly ambivalent. It is difficult not to feel that Hester Prynne is as much Nathaniel Hawthorne as Emma Bovary is Gustave Flaubert. Hester indeed is a Hawthorne-like artist; her embroidery is a metaphor for her creator's narrative art, and the scarlet letter she wears is defiantly an aesthetic artifact, representing art far more truly than it represents adultery, though hardly in the view of Puritan Boston.

Hawthorne's implicit celebration of Hester's sexual nature is also necessarily a celebration of her highly individual will, which is more a post-Emersonian nineteenth-century version of the Protestant will than it is a Puritan kind of seeing, saying, and acting. A Puritan will could not survive isolation; Hester's will belongs to a different order of American spiritual consciousness, one that can find freedom in solitude, even when that solitude is a punishment imposed by a repressive society. Hawthorne informs us that the scarlet letter has "the effect of a spell, taking her out of the ordinary relations with humanity, and enclosing her in a sphere by herself." Since the Puritan public sphere is marked by sadism, hypocrisy, and (as portrayed by Hawthorne with particular skill) a shocking lack of compassion, we can wonder why Hester does not take Pearl and depart into what might be a wholesome exile. The answer, as Hawthorne intimates, is deeply pathetic: Having chosen Dimmesdale, Hester refuses to abandon what she regards as her true marriage. When he dies, his head supported by her bosom, he is still totally unworthy of her, and yet she has remained true to the integrity of her own will.

Biographical Sketch

Nathaniel Hawthorne was born July 4, 1804, the son of Elizabeth Manning Hathorne and Nathaniel Hathorne Sr., who was descended from an interrogator at the Salem witch trials. (Hawthorne added the *w* to his name around 1830). In 1809, after the death of his father, Hawthorne, his mother, and his two sisters lived at the home of his maternal grandparents. His early studies took place at Samuel Archer's School. In his childhood, Hawthorne read extensively in classic literature, absorbing Edmund Spenser's *The Faerie Queene*, John Bunyan's *Pilgrim's Progress*, William Shakespeare, Walter Scott, and endless gothic romances. The sentiments of these works saturate his writing, lending them a sense of self-knowledge, precision, and great insight into human character.

This grounding in literature stood Hawthorne in good stead during his college years at Bowdoin College in Maine, where he joined the Athenean Literary Society and began to write the first of many short stories. His classmates included poet Henry Wadsworth Longfellow and Franklin Pierce, the future president of the United States, who became one of Hawthorne's closest friends. Although he was a mediocre student who could not be bothered to study any topics that did not catch his eye, the years at Bowdoin had an enormous influence on Hawthorne's career.

From Bowdoin, Hawthorne returned to Salem, to the "chamber under the eaves" at his mother's house where he was to spend many solitary years. From 1825 to 1837, Hawthorne perfected his craft, writing tales, sketches, and ideas for novels and poems. During this time he developed the moral universe that would undergird his later works, reading extensively in both classic and contemporary literature and jotting his responses in his voluminous notebooks. He self-published his first novel, *Fanshawe*, based on his Bowdoin years but, embarrassed at his early effort, withdrew the book and destroyed every copy he could find. Two years after the publication of *Fanshawe*, in 1830, Hawthorne published his first short story, "The Hollow of the Three Hills," in the Salem

Gazette. Over the next few years he published several sketches, semiautobiographical works, and tales in various magazines but did not receive any critical or popular attention until he published his first collection of short stories, *Twice-Told Tales*, in 1837; an expanded edition appeared in 1842.

In 1837, Hawthorne, who was famously taciturn, self-contained, and cool in temperament, fell deeply in love. Sophia Peabody was also from Salem, an invalid whose cheerfulness and good temper were unaffected by her illness. She and Hawthorne became secretly engaged, partially because they feared the disapproval of her family and partially because they enjoyed the delicious spark of their hidden relationship. Hawthorne realized that his meager earnings as a writer would not be enough to support Sophie and began lobbying for a political appointment. Since his time at Bowdoin, he had been an ardent supporter of the Democratic Party in which his friend Franklin Pierce was active. Through his connections in government, Hawthorne became the official measurer of coal and salt at the Boston Custom House. Although the post paid well, Hawthorne found that the long hours and physical demands kept him from his writing, and after two years he realized that he had to find another way of supporting himself.

Influenced by Sophia's interest in the transcendentalist movement, Hawthorne invested money in an experimental Utopian community, Brook Farm, and spent a year there before the romance of farming palled. After leaving Brook Farm, Hawthorne devoted himself once again to writing full time in the attic of his family's house. In 1842, he and Sophia were married, and they moved to the Old Manse in Concord, Massachusetts. Their three years there were the happiest time of Hawthorne's life, as he wrote; spent time with Henry David Thoreau, Margaret Fuller, and other writers; and worked in the garden with Sophia. While at the Old Manse, Sophia gave birth to their first child, Una, in 1844; a delicate child, her health was a constant concern to her parents. Una was followed by a brother, Julian, in 1846 and a sister, Rose, in 1851.

Between 1842 and 1846, when he published his second collection of tales, *Mosses from an Old Manse*, Hawthorne worked steadily and published many of his stories in magazines. After a frustrating stint as surveyor of the Salem Custom House, which he describes humorously in the introduction to *The Scarlet Letter*, Hawthorne embarked on the most prolific and successful part of his career.

The Scarlet Letter, Hawthorne's tragic, brilliant tale of passion and retribution, possesses a strength and depth that he was never to achieve in any of his other works. The novel attained immediate public success, both financially and critically, upon its publication in 1850. The overwhelming acclaim invigorated Hawthorne and spurred an astonishing amount of work. In the next two years he wrote *The House of the Seven Gables* (1851), *The Blithedale Romance* (1852), a campaign biography of his friend Franklin Pierce, as well as a collection of tales and two children's books. Even this prodigious output was not enough to support the family, though, and in 1853 he accepted the position of U.S. consul to England from President Franklin Pierce.

The years in England solved Hawthorne's financial problems and introduced him to the glorious art and culture of Europe but dealt a fatal blow to his artistic powers. From 1853 until his death in 1864, he published only one novel, *The Marble Faun* (1860), and a collection of articles and essays, *Our Old Home* (1863). After his post in England, the Hawthornes lived in Rome and Florence from 1857 to 1859 and returned to Concord in 1860, living at his mother's home, the Wayside, until the author's death. Hawthorne was frequently ill and deeply distressed by the looming Civil War that threatened to tear the country apart. Despite the presence of his family, Hawthorne had begun to feel an acute sense of loneliness and loss, an inability to communicate deeply either personally or in his writing. He began work again and again on novels, only to break off in frustration. By March 1864, Sophia was alarmed by his haggard, weak appearance, by the light that had gone out of his eyes. On May 18, 1864, while on a journey to Plymouth, New Hampshire, with Franklin Pierce, Hawthorne died in his sleep, leaving a legacy of imagination and perception unmatched in American fiction.

The Story Behind the Story

"There is evil in every human heart," wrote Nathaniel Hawthorne in his notebooks. In Hawthorne's greatest works, his somber, mysterious, carefully structured prose analyzes the problem of sin inherent in the beautiful and terrible world humans have created; *The Scarlet Letter* is his masterpiece on sin, terrible secrecy, and retribution.

Nathaniel Hawthorne was born on the Fourth of July, 1804, in Salem, Massachusetts, to a family that had resided in Salem for more than a hundred years. Among the men who interrogated those persons brought before the witch court of 1692, the records include a Judge John Hathorne (the family had not yet added the *w* to its surname). Nathaniel Hawthorne chose to write historical fictions, "romances" or semifantastic stories, drawing on New England's past, which also placed him in a strange relationship to these ancestors; he was connected to them in the material and yet detached from them artistically. That he himself would have been criticized harshly by his Puritan forbears for wasting his life writing frivolous stories was not something he doubted. A passage from his notebooks is revealing:

'What is he?' murmurs one gray shadow of my forefathers to the other. 'A writer of story-books! What kind of business in life,—what mode of glorifying God, or being serviceable to mankind in his day and generation,—may that be? Why, the degenerate fellow might as well have been a fiddler!'

In 1846, Hawthorne's friends in the Democratic Party, including future president and Hawthorne's college friend from Bowdoin, Franklin Pierce, nominated him for a surveyor's job at the custom house in Salem. He had tried and failed to support his family through his writing, producing both serious literature and less inspired, less personal, commercial work. His second child, Julian, had just been born, and the family badly needed an income. Unfortunately, Hawthorne acquired his post as the result of a rather heated competition, and his success earned him a number of detractors in the local administration. To complicate matters, he detested the work; while it was not an especially demanding position, Hawthorne felt his post was sapping his creative powers. For the first 18 months of his employment at the custom house, Hawthorne does not appear to have written anything. Eventually, he resumed writing short stories, but progress was slow. Late in 1848, finding short story writing no longer appealed to him, Hawthorne cautiously decided once again to turn his hand to the novel form, which he had not attempted since his failed first novel, *Fanshawe*, 20 years earlier.

As it happened, he would have ample freedom to work on his new project: When the Whigs replaced the Democrats in Washington, early in 1849, Hawthorne lost his post; critics speculate that the heated political arena he found himself in contributed to his acrimonious tone in *The Scarlet Letter*. Hawthorne lost more than his job in 1849—he also lost his mother. He had been a dutiful son, and her death was an especially heavy blow to him. By the end of the year, he had relocated his family to Lenox, Massachusetts. It was during this time, between his departure from the custom house and his departure from Salem, that *The Scarlet Letter* was composed.

The novel was a surprising literary and commercial success when it first appeared in 1850, selling out its first run in just 10 days. Even halfway into the nineteenth century, American literary markets were dominated by English imports, and American writers were still struggling to establish a distinctly American literary idiom. The New York–based group of writers and editors known as Young America began to promote Hawthorne's work as an example of a new and distinctly American literary style. It was largely through their attentions that Hawthorne was introduced to Herman Melville, who wrote an ardently affirmative review of *Mosses from an Old Manse* for *Literary World*, comparing Hawthorne favorably to Shakespeare. This review, along with the popularity of *The Scarlet Letter*, helped to solidify Hawthorne's reputation as an important American writer, as one of the first members of an American canon.

Henry James, one of the most important writers of the generation succeeding Hawthorne's, wrote the first substantial treatise on his work. "*The Scarlet Letter*," he writes, "contains little enough of gaiety or hopefulness. It is densely dark, with a single spot of vivid colour in it; and it will probably long remain the most consistently gloomy of English novels of the first order. But I just now called it the author's masterpiece, and I imagine it will continue to be, for other generations than ours, his most substantial title to fame." History proved James right, as *The Scarlet Letter* has become one of the most commonly read and best-known nineteenth-century American novels.

List of Characters

Hester Prynne
Born in England to a once noble family, Hester was consigned to a loveless marriage of convenience with Master Prynne, later known as Roger Chillingworth. After a brief season in Amsterdam, it was decided that they would join the Puritans in Boston; Hester ventured across the Atlantic first, her husband planning to join her later. After roughly a year, during which time she had received no word of her husband, and many speculated he had died en route to America, Hester committed adultery with the local minister, Arthur Dimmesdale. She became pregnant, and so the crime was discovered and punished. A stately, robust, and darkly beautiful woman, she seems to retain some of the grace and poise of the aristocracy from which she is descended; and she perhaps resembles her ancestors in her self-reliance and confidence in her own conscience. Hester exhibits immense strength of character during the course of the novel's events, accepting her punishment without resentment and without resigning her authority over herself, even over her own sin. She becomes a benefactor to the community that has judged her sternly and ostracized her for a not incomprehensible crime; she becomes a sign and a prophet, as well, to the Puritan community of Boston, accumulating different interpretations as time goes by. Hester is severely tested, not so much by the gross cruelty of her community toward her but by her concern over the fate of Pearl, her daughter. Her noble resolve not to expose Dimmesdale nevertheless places Pearl in moral jeopardy. By the end of the novel, she is desperate enough to agree to run away to Europe with Dimmesdale and live with him in sin.

Roger Chillingworth
Hester Prynne's husband, the slightly deformed Master Prynne, had dedicated his youth to study, only to find middle age lonelier than he had expected. Longing for a family, his eye settled on young Hester, and they were married. Having sent

Hester to America in advance of his arrival, Prynne came shortly thereafter, only to be taken and held captive for a year by native peoples. Upon emerging at last from the forest, he discovers his wife being held up to public opprobrium for adultery; to avoid humiliation, and to better facilitate his search for the father of his wife's illegitimate child, he adopts the name "Roger Chillingworth." While he is able to forgive Hester, who promises to protect the secret of his identity as closely as she does that of her lover, he cannot bring himself to forgive the man who has wronged them both. In time, having set himself up as a doctor in Boston, he artfully discovers the true culprit and sets himself the task of hounding and provoking Dimmesdale's racked conscience into morbid and ultimately life-threatening personal torture. He perverts the purposes of medicine, seeking to prolong life only as a means of extending suffering. By adopting the role of Dimmesdale's self-appointed tormentor, Chillingworth unwittingly sets in motion his own decline. As the novel draws to a close, he is only the withered husk of the nobler man he had formerly been.

Arthur Dimmesdale

The minister for the town of Boston, Arthur Dimmesdale was educated in England, bringing with him to America a great power of persuasive speech, extensive learning, and a simple, almost angelic faith. Where Chillingworth possesses an invasive, penetrating eye, Dimmesdale has a soft yet penetrating voice; he does not hector and terrify his congregation in the course of his sermons but persuades and inspires them. Dimmesdale is handsome and, drawn as much by her inner nobility as by her outward beauty, commits adultery with Hester Prynne, who bears his child. He does not confess his crime to the community he serves in order to continue his good work, and, in fact, his secret sin makes him an even more effective minister; unlike all the other Puritan authorities, he is unable to sit in complacent judgment of others. Instead of facing public condemnation, Dimmesdale punishes himself in private, subjecting himself to torments—made worse by Chillingworth—that are ultimately far more damaging than the official punishment he would have otherwise faced. He is not exactly a hypocrite, since, in the first place, the Puritan religion regards all people to be sinners unworthy of salvation, and, in the second place, he does not deceive himself into believing in his innocence. In this regard, he stands in stark contrast to such characters as Governor Bellingham, who is callous and unforgiving in the name of Christianity. Dimmesdale, by preventing the Boston authorities from taking Pearl away from her, saves Hester from the damning temptation to hate and seek revenge on the community. Finally, as he feels his life ebbing away, Dimmesdale makes his confession and saves Pearl as well.

Pearl Prynne

Pearl is the only major character in the novel to be born in America. Born in prison and several months old before ever seeing broad daylight, she is an otherworldly, fairylike, or implike child, a fatherless changeling who is seemingly not fully human. A graceful girl of uncannily perfect beauty, but with an unruly, mercurial personality, she has the potential to become monstrous or to develop into a worthy human being. Conceived during a period in Hester's life of profound interior warfare, Pearl came into the world with these elements of strife contained or admixed in her: She is their embodiment. While not a cold or unloving child, she cannot fail to resent her mother's refusal to tell her who her father is. Pearl, however, cannot be fooled; she instinctively perceives Chillingworth's demonical malice and seems to understand that Dimmesdale is her father, even if she cannot understand why no one will confirm that he is. When he finally acknowledges her before all of Boston, the spell that kept her from being entirely human is broken, and she is able to weep for him, exhibiting the empathy that was formerly absent in her.

Summary and Analysis

The Scarlet Letter opens with an extended, semiautobiographical preface, which serves the book less as an overture than as a bridge linking the past, as portrayed in Hawthorne's narrative, to the present and to the modern art of self-referential techniques associated with modern and postmodern fiction. *The Scarlet Letter* is not a record of historical fact, but it draws from history; the scarlet letter that Hester Prynne wears is embroidered with gold thread, and likewise the historical information that Hawthorne draws upon to write his novel is embroidered with fictional events. These events, however, do not simply exploit history for background material; rather, they test our understanding of that past history and attempt to resurrect from dry facts a living picture of the past in all its moral complexity. The study of history teaches us that each generation judges the one preceding it according to the standards of its own time and place and not according to the standards of that previous time. This judgment, therefore, is an anachronism if not an unjust assessment. Hawthorne instead advocates a subtler, more sophisticated approach; he tries to revive the past and examine it in the light of the present as though the past were able to answer the present's allegations with its own voice. Hawthorne tries to show that the circumstances and conditions of past times were different. Most important of all, he tries to show that a reductive moral judgment about the past tells us nothing new; it merely reaffirms in the present what we already know.

Just as Hawthorne has embroidered history to give us the scarlet letter, he also embroiders his own autobiography in the preface. Hawthorne took a job at Salem's Custom House in 1846. The custom house, he suggests, is run in the same thoughtless, convention-bound way that prevailed in Puritan Boston. Some of the employees are almost old enough to remember Puritan Boston. Hawthorne invents a predecessor, Jonathan Pue, who is supposed to have written an imaginary record of the events in Hester Prynne's case. He even describes finding the scarlet letter itself, lying among Pue's documents. So, the account of the origin of the novel is also fictional. History is a collection of stories human beings tell about themselves to one another and to those who will come after them; facts are involved in these accounts, but they have a personal and philosophical significance that far outweighs the objective importance of these facts. A significance emerges when one reads history critically but without rushing to judgment.

The Scarlet Letter is a novel about judgment and about the relations that arise between publicly trumpeted or imposed values and private moral decision. It is important to make this point at once, because *The Scarlet Letter* is too often imprecisely read as a condemnation of Puritan hypocrisy and intolerance; these are matters of concern for Hawthorne, but they are not the principal focus of the narrative. The Puritans provide an excellent example of provincial bigotry and unself-conscious inconsistency between theory and practice; Hawthorne does depict them, for the most part, as ignorant rabble. However, their hypocrisy and prejudice are not entirely taken for granted; rather, they are tested by the events of the novel and permitted to unfold in a variety of opinions. Even the vulgar Boston Puritans are not perfectly uniform; a plurality of opinion on a number of subjects and gradual changes in opinion are evident among them.

Hawthorne commonly deals with moral crises that have both a cut-and-dry aspect on the one hand and a considerably more vague aspect on the other. Hester Prynne is definitely guilty of adultery, and, while the crime is unfortunate, it is not abominable. Despite the many mitigating circumstances, it is never represented as less than a crime—in fact, when Hester and Dimmesdale are tempted to run away together, the impulse is represented as a moment of serious moral jeopardy. However firmly established Hester's guilt may be, such that the cause of her guilt is established as fact and may not be tampered with, the effects of her guilt introduce many ambiguities. As a result of her crime and her punishment, she becomes a great asset to the community, greater than she might otherwise have been.

21

Dimmesdale becomes a more effective minister as a result of his secret guilt; the essential flaw in Hester's marriage is brought plainly into view.

As is usual with Hawthorne's novels, the plot is straightforward, with a minimum of events, dealing in the main with the interaction of characters in a basically fixed, many-layered predicament. It is set in Boston in the time of the Puritans. Hester Prynne is a beautiful young woman of formerly aristocratic stock; a Puritan born in England, she married a studious older man she neither loved nor pretended to love, for reasons that are largely implied (he was lonely; he took notice of her; somehow the marriage was arranged). Like the Pilgrims who settled the Plymouth Colony in 1620, she and her husband moved to the Netherlands for a time and then made plans to resettle in America. Hester is sent ahead of her husband, who then fails to arrive or to send any word. As time passes, she begins to suspect some mischance has waylaid him, perhaps a shipwreck, and that he may be dead. After roughly a year, she commits adultery with Arthur Dimmesdale, the young minister of Boston; their crime is more a mutual lapse than a matter of wickedness or defiance to society. Plainly, the two would make a happily married couple, if she were free.

Hester becomes pregnant, and her crime cannot long be concealed. She is put in prison, where she gives birth to a baby girl, Pearl Prynne. Although she is pressured by town officials to reveal the identity of the child's father, she refuses to do so. Dimmesdale, while bitterly tormented by guilt and sympathy for Hester's suffering, does not reveal his parentage; were he to be exposed, he could no longer serve the community as its minister, something he is amply able to do. Unlike the other Puritan ministers of the time, Dimmesdale is not a stentorian dogmatist loudly condemning sin but a more spiritual, uplifting sermonizer. His work in Boston clearly demonstrates that he is a man of superior abilities and deep faith who possesses a rare capacity for self-sacrifice. It is precisely this aspect of his character that makes him most susceptible to anguish for Hester's suffering and his own sin. It also enables him to marvel at Hester's extraordinary strength of character and to appreciate in full her sacrifice for him.

The novel opens with "**The Prison Door**," a brief chapter of three paragraphs that sets the scene by means of an extended description of a single, symbolic element. This is the reader's first encounter with Hawthorne's Puritan Boston: "a throng of bearded men, in sad-colored garments and gray" and waiting for the door to their small prison house to open. The prison door separates the prisoners from the free citizens, the jail from the town; observing this scene, it is not immediately clear on which side of the door the Puritans are grouped. Immediately at the outset, and with considerable elegance, Hawthorne has established a double standard, such that the judgment of the Puritans is never represented without the suggestion of a contrary viewpoint. No one in Hawthorne's fiction is free to judge another; in putting up a heavy prison door "studded with iron spikes," they have bound themselves as much as they have bound their prisoners.

Before proceeding to the story, Hawthorne draws the reader's attention to a rose bush, growing among the plants surrounding the prison. As some had suggested about its origin, "it had sprung up under the footsteps of the sainted Ann Hutchinson, as she entered the prison-door." Ann Hutchinson was an early antinomian, believing she was bound to the laws solely of God and not of society. She was persecuted by the Boston Puritans in the first years of the Massachussetts Bay Company's existence for rejecting their judgmental and austere moral theology. After spending time in jail, she was expelled from the colony and eventually killed in a massacre by Native Americans in New Rochelle, New York. Hawthorne explains that this story transpires 15 or 20 years after the founding of Boston, which places the date between 1645 and 1650. Ann Hutchinson had been gone for no less than 12 years.

The prison door opens, and the second chapter, "**The Market-Place**," begins. To a casual observer, Hawthorne explains, the grim demeanor of the Puritans would suggest that the perpetrator of some drastic crime was about to appear, when, in fact, such dourness is commonplace, and Puritanical discipline is often so severe that even minor infractions, or differences of opinion in religious matters, are a matter of deep moral gravity to them. Hester Prynne will meet with no sympathy for her crime, but, on the other hand, she will not be mocked for her shame. In passing, Hawthorne mentions Mistress Hibbins, widow of the magistrate, who is widely rumored to be a witch—we will encounter her again later. The women of Puritan Boston are of "a coarser fibre" than women in Hawthorne's own time; they are hardworking and blunt talking. Their disapproval of Hester is especially strong; some of the women exhibit signs of jealousy of Hester, without realizing it themselves, and from this group comes the most vehement judgment.

Hester's much-anticipated first appearance then occurs, and it is important to take careful note of the manner in which Hawthorne presents her. The beadle (a sort of policeman and warder in one) draws her toward the door with his hand on her shoulder. Just within the door, she puts his hand off, "by an action marked with natural dignity and force of character" and emerges from the jail on her own, "as if by her own free will." She is carrying Pearl, her daughter, who is seeing the light of day for the first time; she holds Pearl in such a way as to conceal the letter on her chest, the embroidered *A*, for "adultress." Pearl and the letter will be associated closely throughout the novel, so it is not insignificant that they each appear at the same time. Hester shifts her grasp on Pearl so as not to hide the letter, "with a burning blush, and yet a haughty smile, and a glance that would not be abashed." Being an expert seamstress, Hester has embroidered the letter and included "fantastic flourishes of gold thread." She has transformed the mark of shame into a rich ornament. In her and her actions, there is a profound mixture of shame and defiance. Hester accepts the law, the charge, and the punishment, but she refuses to be replaced by them. Her destiny will remain her own to determine, and she has not resigned her rights as a human being.

Hawthorne describes Hester's appearance; she is a sturdy and beautiful woman. Later in the chapter, she remembers her childhood home in England, with its "half-obliterated shield of arms over the portal, in token of antique gentility." Hester is therefore the descendent of a once noble line and perhaps retains some of her ancestors' native poise and dignity of bearing—and sense of self-worth.

Hester is led to the platform in the marketplace and exposed to the crowd. She must stand there and allow them to stare at her, to impose and impress their disapproval onto her. Hawthorne explains that, while Hester has the strength to bear insult, this demeaning public display taxes her to the utmost limit of her emotional endurance. Her mind takes refuge in images of the past, and in the process the reader is introduced to the bare facts of her case: her marriage in England to an old scholarly man whose left shoulder is "a trifle higher than the right" and their subsequent removal to "a Continental city" (Amsterdam).

In "**The Recognition,**" a new figure is introduced. Emerging from the wilderness, accompanied by a native guide, comes a small man "with a furrowed visage" and one shoulder higher than the other. This is her husband, who has chosen an extremely awkward day on which to rejoin his wife. Hester and her husband recognize each other, and a silent drama is played out within them. Feigning only casual interest, Master Prynne asks a bystander about Hester as though she were a stranger and discovers the circumstances of her shame. She is standing not only in the presence of the crowd but before the governor of the colony and its chief religious authorities as well, all of whom are deficient in mustering or offering sympathy. John Wilson, the most revered minister in the colony, exhorts Hester to reveal her lover's name, even placing his hand on Dimmesdale's shoulder as he does so. Before we are introduced to Dimmesdale directly, we learn that he has opposed any attempt to force Hester to name Pearl's father.

Arthur Dimmesdale is everything the other Puritan authorities are not; he is young, sensitive, sympathetic, tenderly spiritual, and wholly lacking in cruel instincts. Whereas Wilson and Bellingham are like stern, unforgiving Old Testament prophets, Dimmesdale is like an angel or a child. Wilson commands Dimmesdale to speak to Hester, and he issues his first speech in the novel; he urges her to answer, saying, "Be not silent from any mistaken pity and tenderness for him; for, believe me, Hester, though he were to step down from a high place, and stand there beside thee, on thy pedestal of shame, yet better were it so, than to hide a guilty heart through life." Just as the words of the other Puritan leaders provoke the crowd's impulse to judge and condemn, so Dimmesdale's words bring "the listeners into one accord of sympathy."

Why does Hester preserve Dimmesdale's secret? Clearly she does so, in part, out of respect for his good works, but more so because, in asserting her own free will, she must assert the free will of all. She cannot confess on someone else's behalf, no matter how tempting the prospect; Dimmesdale must confess on his own. It is not Hester's decision to make, nor is it fair for Dimmesdale to impose it on her. She refuses, at great personal cost, to answer. Not only does she lose all chance of removing the scarlet letter from her chest, but she throws away Pearl's only opportunity to know her true father. " . . . my child must seek a heavenly Father; she shall never know an earthly one!" After a fire-and-brimstone sermon from Wilson, Hester, who has lapsed into a kind of steely deliriousness in the course of her ordeal, is returned to the prison.

The next chapter is "**The Interview**." Once out of the public eye, Hester lapses into a state of intense emotional distress, and, as a man of science, who but her husband is called to attend her. Introducing himself as Roger Chillingworth, he asks to be left alone with Hester; with the jailer out of the way, they are free to drop the pretense of being strangers to each other. He provides a drug for Pearl, who has also become distraught; when Hester hesitates to administer it, her husband answers, "What should ail me to harm this misbegotten and miserable babe?" The drug proves to be effective, and Chillingworth then concocts a potion for his wife: "Even if I imagine a scheme of vengeance, what could I do better for my object than to let thee live,—than to give thee medicines against all harm and peril of life,—so that this burning shame may still blaze upon thy bosom?" This is the equivocal key to

Chillingworth's character; he is a doctor who heals and harms at once. His excellence in medicine is a sign of malice or cold curiosity, not of sympathy or compassion.

All the same, he does not ultimately blame or despise Hester for her crime. "It was my folly, and thy weakness . . . from the moment when we came down the old church-steps together, a married pair, I might have beheld the bale-fire of that scarlet letter blazing at the end of our path!" Mismatched in age and inclination, the couple had little chance of forming a successful partnership. Hester, though little inclined to defend herself, points out that she "felt no love, nor feigned any" for her husband who had grown cold and aloof through excessive study. Chillingworth grants the point; he, like Faust, found himself old and alone after many decades of study and attempted to foster, before it was too late, a loving family. He accepts his failure and promises Hester he has no intention of trying to avenge himself on her. In regard to her lover, however, he has no such magnanimous feelings; he presses her to confess his name, but she will not. Chillingworth is unfazed; while he has been compelled to accept his failure as a husband, he still has complete confidence in his powers of observation, even of detection. He is certain he will find out the identity of Hester's lover and find his own way to punish him. In the meantime, he is willing to bargain with Hester; if she will not tell him the name of her lover, she may at least bind herself to a similar promise with regard to Chillingworth's true identity. In this way, Hester's social isolation will be reinforced by multiple obligations to conceal the truth of two identities, and, in so doing, she will undermine the identity of her own daughter, Pearl.

In chapter 5, "**Hester and Her Needle,**" the more outrageous test of her mettle being over, daily trials begin for the protagonist. Hester is now free to leave the prison, but her everyday life is hardly to be preferred to confinement. The scarlet letter is a burden she will wear until her death, and in life, "giving up her individuality, she would become the general symbol at which the preacher and moralist might point, in which they might vivify and embody their images of woman's frailty and sinful passion." Of course, she might simply choose to leave New England; but Hawthorne explains that Hester is so completely transformed by her ordeal that it is as if she were born anew into the world and bound by her very sin to the environs of Boston. This is not all. Hester's motive for remaining, at least as she explains it to herself, is "half a truth, half a self-delusion." She believes that, by remaining, she has some hope of redeeming herself; but, without acknowledging it, she also remains because she cannot bear to part from Dimmesdale. He alone in the world can share her shame, can understand her suffering. She regards herself to be "connected in a union" with him—to be, in fact, his true wife. Hawthorne had, in his own way, a sharp understanding of what psychologists would later term the unconscious. His characters frequently act on motives that they do not correctly or clearly perceive; and Hawthorne has no qualms about pointing to and plainly stating these motives for the benefit of his readers.

Hester and Pearl take up residence in a modest, isolated home on the outskirts of town. While the land there is barren, and the prospects poor, Hester is blessed with exceptional skill in embroidery. It is she, the rejected outcast, who makes the fine lace that adorns the colony's officials at state occasions—and departed loved ones in their coffins—and, most ironically of all, her linen is in high demand among the citizenry's "legitimate" offspring. Even Governor Bellingham himself wears some of Hester's needlework on his ruff. "But it is not recorded that, in a single instance, her skill was called in aid to embroider the white veil which was to cover the pure blushes of a bride. The exception indicated the ever relentless vigor with which society frowned upon her sin." In any event, Hester is able to earn a meager living.

While Hester herself wears only the plainest clothes, Pearl, as the years pass, is dressed with "a fantastic ingenuity." Hester has not only skill but vision and taste when it comes to creating garments; her work is considered beautiful. Furthermore, even though she herself is not far from poverty, Hester gives money to the poor, even to those who are better off than she, and spends her time fashioning simple clothing for them. In short,

Hester is determined to contribute to Boston society, whether the Puritans of Boston like it or not. This resolve is all the more remarkable in light of the fact that "Every gesture, every word, and even the silence of those with whom she came in contact, implied, and often expressed, that she was banished. . . ." Worst of all, her experience of sin has made her more sympathetically sensitive to it, so that she seems able, almost magically, to detect bad conscience when confronted with it. Hester finds herself compelled to convince herself repeatedly that the people around her are not all sinners like her, or perhaps worse.

The reader is meant to understand that time is passing, that Hawthorne is describing typical events as they play out in the years following Hester's sentencing. Pearl is growing into a young girl, into a character in the novel, and we find out more about her in the chapter "**Pearl.**" Hester regards Pearl with great misgivings: "She knew that her deed had been evil; she could have no faith, therefore, that its result would be for good." She observes Pearl's growth and development with concern and finds her a disturbingly remote, unsympathetic girl. Not exactly cold, Pearl experiences whimsical delight as well as truly violent rage; but there is no love in her. She possesses grace and a mercurial personality and is potentially wild and unruly. Rules and discipline are meaningless to her, yet she is not malicious. Hester is frightened by Pearl's strangeness; she finds her daughter unintelligible, an enigma. Time and again Hawthorne compares Pearl to a fairy child, a changeling, an imp, or witch-child. Pearl is not fully human, because she does not experience rooted human emotions; it is as though she lives in a dream. When Hester musingly asks her, " . . . whence didst thou come?" Pearl replies, "It is thou that must tell me!" While Pearl cannot entirely understand her situation, she already knows that her mother is hiding something from her.

As is made clear later in the novel, roughly three years have passed since the events that opened the novel. In "**The Governor's Hall**," Hester presents herself to Governor Bellingham, ostensibly to deliver to him a pair of gloves he has ordered but also to discover if there is any truth to the rumor that official proceedings are underfoot that, if successful, will take Pearl away from her. "Some of the leading inhabitants" of the colony are of the opinion that Hester is a bad influence on Pearl, or possibly vice-versa; in any event, Governor Bellingham appears to be of their party. Hester brings Pearl with her to the Governor's Hall. Dressed in livid red, Pearl appears to be "the scarlet letter endowed with life" and so the theme of Pearl's identification with the letter is deepened and extended in this chapter. Pearl is therefore both the chief recipient of Hester's love and the emblem of her crime. Some Puritan children take it into their heads to assault Pearl, hurling mud at her, but Pearl routs them fiercely; it is not possible to intimidate her.

Hester gains admission to the governor's somberly luxurious house, filled with ponderous, rich items brought from England. The walls of the main hall are lined with portraits of Bellingham's ancestors, as grim and cheerless as the family's current representative. Also on display is the governor's suit of polished armor, reflecting the dazzling rays of the sun. At Pearl's urging, Hester regards her reflection in the breastplate. The curved surface so distorts her appearance that she seems to vanish behind the scarlet letter; clearly, the distorted perspective of the reflection in the governor's armor is a figure for the exaggeratedly stern and steely point of view of the man himself. Whenever dealing with Puritan subjects, Hawthorne often makes use of their armor as a way of indicating their rigidity and warlike attitude toward the world. They are so wary of injury to their souls that they can be symbolically seen as willingly confining themselves cramped in an emotional and spiritual armor as heavy and cumbersome as the actual suit adorning the residence. In addition, the Puritan vision of the world is also affected by this rigid self-control, so that all the bright notes are dulled, and happiness is disdained or ignored, while sin and the inevitable judgment of a vengeful God on the sinner are emphasized until they alone are visible. Pearl's appearance is altered as well by the armor: In its light and presence, she seems to become a leering imp, a monster.

Shaken by what she has seen, Hester leads Pearl to the window, where they look out over the governor's garden. Pearl wants one of the governor's red roses; we are reminded not only of her own red garment and the significance of that color but also of the rose bush that grew outside the prison door. At this point, the governor and the various important persons with whom he has been meeting appear on the garden path.

The scene continues in "**The Elf-Child and the Minister.**" Governor Bellingham and John Wilson are the first of the procession in the garden. While they are stern Puritans, neither man denies himself a degree of private luxury that is not entirely commensurate with their public asperity. Arthur Dimmesdale walks behind them, in the company of Roger Chillingworth, who has become his doctor. Dimmesdale's health has been deteriorating, possibly due to overwork, and Chillingworth is treating him; both of them have visibly altered—Dimmesdale is "careworn and emaciated" and as always "pale," while Chillingworth has become "uglier," "duskier," and "more misshapen." The governor, entering his house, sees Pearl standing alone by the door—Hester being momentarily concealed in shadow. He remarks on Pearl's outlandish attire and compares her to the "children of the Lord of Misrule." This is a reference to certain English holiday customs, in which the appointed "lord" is free to parody the vaunting manners of the aristocracy, and the normal social order is playfully turned on its head. Pearl, as a child of the Lord of Misrule, would be a sort of aberration, a figure of mischief. John Wilson, in a spirit of dour raillery, asks Pearl if she is "a Christian child" or a fairy. Upon telling them her name, Wilson responds she would be better named for something red, "Ruby, rather!—or Coral!—or Red Rose, at the very least, judging from thy hue!" One must note again that Pearl is being compared to the roses; like them, she can be both pristine and dangerous.

Noting Hester's presence, and whose child Pearl therefore is, the governor is not so gallant as to refrain from calling Hester "a worthy type of her of Babylon"—a prostitute, in other words. He accosts Hester, asking what she could possibly have to teach her child for the salvation of her soul. Hester points to the letter and says "I can teach my little Pearl what I have learned from this!" The two venerable men decide to test

Pearl; Reverend Wilson begins to catechize her, but, although Pearl has been exposed to religious teaching by Hester, she perversely refuses to speak. When they ask her who made her, she insists she was originally a rose, growing on the rose bush by the prison door. Here again is the willful conflation, on Pearl's part, of the question of her relationship to her heavenly father, the creator of whom the minister and the governor are speaking, and her relationship to her unknown biological father.

Pearl's apparent ignorance seems to indict Hester as a bad mother, but she, desperate not to lose the only thing left to her in the world, forcefully defends her right to keep Pearl. She even turns to Dimmesdale for help, indirectly and unobtrusively invoking his share in her downfall as reason to intervene on her behalf. Dimmesdale, with his habitual sweetness and eloquence, in a voice that is at once soft and yet so "powerful . . . that the hall reëchoed, and the hollow armour rang with it," argues that Hester must be allowed to keep Pearl. God has sent her this child as a blessing and a curse, a lesson to be learned through love, and a means "to keep the mother's soul alive." He means that, had Hester been left with nothing, in bitterness and despair she might have embraced evil ways or taken her own life (a sin, even among non-Puritans). Dimmesdale makes a convincing case, but his emotional investment in Hester's defense does not go unnoticed by Chillingworth, who is beginning to suspect that Dimmesdale's connection to Hester and Pearl may be more than it appears to be.

As is often the case, Pearl responds to the situation with an uncanny sense of the truth but without being able to see it or name it for what it is. Dimmesdale's words have somehow reached her elusive heart, and she gently rubs his hand with her cheek in a rare show of human warmth. Ultimately, the governor and John Wilson decide to leave the matter for the time being and wait to see how things develop. Hester will keep Pearl for the time being. The chapter, however, is not over. As she leaves the Governor's Hall, Hester exchanges words with Mistress Hibbins, the governor's sister and a witch. She asks Hester if she will come to her witch's sabbath that night, and

Hester replies, "I must tarry at home, and keep watch over my little Pearl. Had they taken her from me, I would willingly have gone with thee into the forest, and signed my name in the Black Man's book too, and that with mine own blood!" In other words, Hester is confirming Dimmesdale's suspicion, that without Pearl, she would have abandoned all hope of redemption and even of Christian charity. She would have become a witch: a malefactor, rather than a benefactor, to her community.

With the ninth chapter, "**The Leech**," Hawthorne redirects the reader's attention away from Hester Prynne. Roger Chillingworth is the first real doctor and man of science to practice in Boston, and his medical knowledge is supplemented by a thoroughgoing familiarity with the magical principles of alchemy, and with native lore, acquired during his long captivity. He is associated with supernatural knowledge, a faculty of perceiving hidden and secret things. Detecting the sudden degeneration of Dimmesdale's health and sensing something else—perhaps some small clue as to its real cause—he presses his medical services on the minister. Doctors at this time were often referred to as leeches, since they often employed actual leeches in the treatment of patients; drawing blood was one of the most commonly employed remedies. Chillingworth is a leech in both senses of the word: He is a doctor, and he is a parasite. The two men become uncomfortable intimates. Chillingworth attends Dimmesdale nearly at all times and observes his every action. "He deemed it essential, it would seem, to know the man, before attempting to do him good." Yet he is doing more than acquainting himself with Dimmesdale's habits and character: He is digging into Dimmesdale, trying to take him apart. There is a veiled aggression in Chillingworth's examinations of Dimmesdale, of which perhaps neither man is fully aware. Chillingworth is, apparently, not fully aware of his own suspicions in regard to Dimmesdale; his all-seeing eye proves ironically incapable of turning its gaze back on himself.

The two men end up living under the same roof, and, as they cohabitate, Chillingworth's unconscious bitterness becomes increasingly intense, so much so that he is physically altered by it. Rumors begin to circulate to the effect "that the Reverend Arthur Dimmesdale, like many other person of especial sanctity, in all ages of the Christian world, was haunted either by Satan himself, or Satan's emissary, in the guise of old Roger Chillingworth."

Having provided the background information, Hawthorne then moves to a particular scene involving Dimmesdale and Chillingworth in chapter 10, **"The Leech and His Patient."** Having deftly brought the conversation round to the subject of unconfessed sin, Chillingworth asks Dimmesdale why a man would refuse to confess his crimes. Dimmesdale responds in the general sense but indirectly shedding light on the reasons for his own silence: " . . . guilty as they may be, retaining, nevertheless, a zeal for God's glory and man's welfare, they shrink from displaying themselves black and filthy in the view of men; because, thenceforward, no good can be achieved by them, no evil of the past redeemed by better service." Chillingworth answers that one cannot serve God with "unclean hands" or deny "the shame that rightfully belongs to them."

This conversation transpires by a window in the home Chillingworth and Dimmesdale share; Pearl and Hester then appear in the graveyard outside. Pearl has decorated her mother's letter with burdock burrs and, seeing Dimmesdale, throws one at him. All the main characters momentarily confront one another, then Pearl leads her mother away through the graves. Something in this moment draws Chillingworth closer to a conscious conclusion about Dimmesdale; he inquires after the minister's health, wondering if perhaps he knows everything there is to know—physical diseases sometimes having spiritual causes. Chillingworth asks Dimmesdale if he will unburden his spiritual troubles to him, and Dimmesdale recoils, refusing. " . . . not to an earthly physician!" he cries.

Shortly after this minor confrontation, Dimmesdale falls asleep in his chair. Chillingworth enters the room and, in a gentle but terrible moment of trespass, opens Dimmesdale's clothing and peers at his bare chest. Hawthorne has been careful to note several times Dimmesdale's unconscious habit of pressing his hand to his breast when especially troubled, and so it is clear that his illness is related to his chest, the region of his heart. What Chillingworth sees when he looks at Dimmesdale's naked chest is not revealed to us, the readers, but Chillingworth's reaction is: He turns away

> . . . with what a wild look of wonder, joy, and horror! With what a ghastly rapture, as it were, too mighty to be expressed only by the eye and features, and therefore bursting forth through the whole ugliness of his figure. . . . Had a man seen old Roger Chillingworth, at that moment of his ecstasy, he would have had no need to ask how Satan comports himself, when a precious human soul is lost to heaven, and won into his kingdom.

Because we know Roger Chillingworth has dedicated himself exclusively to the task of discovering the identity of Hester's lover, there is only one plausible interpretation of this scene: Something he has seen on Dimmesdale's chest has convinced him, completely and in a single moment, that Dimmesdale is the man he has been seeking.

In "**The Interior of a Heart**," Hawthorne addresses the question of Chillingworth's subtle motivations. He wants to become as close to Dimmesdale as possible, so as to see as much as he can of Dimmesdale's terrible self-torment; he wants to relish Dimmesdale's suffering as his own revenge. Having discovered the minister's secret, Chillingworth is able to torture him at will—"The victim was for ever on the rack . . ."—while maintaining an outward appearance of complete innocence, even benevolence.

Nonetheless, even in the midst of his suffering, "the Reverend Mr. Dimmesdale had achieved a brilliant popularity in his sacred office. He won it, indeed, in great part, by his sorrows." Dimmesdale is a better minister for being a sinner and a sufferer; his already considerable powers of sympathy are further extended. Unlike his counterparts in the ministry, such as John Wilson, Dimmesdale is not an inflexible, judgmental moralist; he is understanding, forgiving, merciful, reverent, and respectful. Unfortunately, the warm regard he receives in return for his works only exacerbates his guilt and suffering further. There have been times when he tries to confess from the pulpit, but, in calling himself a sinner, "an abomination," he only impresses the congregation all that much more favorably with his modesty and the severity of his moral self-judgment. Desperate for some means to relieve the intolerable burden of his guilt, he resorts to private, secret self-punishment, lashing his own back with a whip and denying himself sleep.

"**The Minister's Vigil**" relates a midnight excursion to the market square, the scene of Hester's humiliation. This is the first time in the course of the narrative that Hawthorne draws us directly into Dimmesdale's presence, having kept him at a distance until such time when Dimmesdale's share in Hester's downfall could be implied if not revealed. Arriving at the platform on which Hester had stood, Dimmesdale climbs it himself, unseen at the midnight hour. He feels as though he bears a scarlet letter over his own heart, where "there had long been, the gnawing and poisonous tooth of bodily pain," and, unable to contain himself, he cries out in anguish. Only two persons respond to his cry—the governor thrusts his head out his window, holding a lantern, but cannot see Dimmesdale in the dark. The witch, Mistress Hibbins, likewise peers out of her window and up at the sky, apparently thinking some demon had passed overhead. Both retire again after a few moments.

Then a light appears in the dark; John Wilson himself, having just attended at the death bed of Governor Winthrop, is passing, on his way back home. Dimmesdale thinks to call out to him but does not, and Wilson passes without seeing him. Alone again, Dimmesdale imagines standing in the square until the morning light discloses his presence to all, thereby forcing his confession. Pearl's mocking laughter breaks his reverie; Hester has also been attending the dying governor and is also on her way home in the dark. Dimmesdale calls to them to join him on the platform, and the three of them are united, alone. Pearl asks if he will stand there with them the next day at noon, but Dimmesdale demurs; he claims they will stand together another time, on judgment day. Then there is a flash of light in the sky—a meteor but, to Dimmesdale, it seems as though a gigantic red *A* appears directly overhead. With equal abruptness, Roger Chillingworth appears, watching them. He is the third person to come from the governor's deathbed. Dimmesdale, terrified, asks, "Who is that man, Hester?" Hester, keeping her promise, does not answer. In this scene, Hawthorne shows us that there are two sides to Dimmesdale's deception; he is also a victim, in that Chillingworth's power over him depends on Dimmesdale's continued concealment of his guilt and on Hester's refusal to reveal who Chillingworth actually is. Pearl offers to tell Dimmesdale who Chillingworth is but only babbles nonsense into his ear. "Dost thou mock me now?" he asks her, to which she replies, "Thou wast not bold!—thou wast not true! . . . Thou wouldst not promise to take my hand, and mother's hand, to-morrow noontide!" Pearl, as usual, unerringly points to the wrong done to her and uses it as a pretext to deny love or compassion to others.

In **"Another View of Hester,"** the narrative focus shifts to Hester and Pearl. Meditating on her encounter with Dimmesdale, Hester is shocked at how compromised his health and mental strength appear to be, and she resolves to offer him whatever help she can. We learn that roughly seven years have elapsed since the opening of the novel. In this time, the animosity directed at Hester has softened and eroded, and the people of Boston have come to regard her in a mixed light. Her charity, goodness, and submission to the judgment against her have not gone unnoticed; many regard the *A* on her breast to mean "angel," in light of the many good works she has done. While the ministers and colonial authorities continue to employ her as a symbol and an object lesson, "individuals in private life, meanwhile, had quite forgiven Hester Prynne for her frailty." Yet Hester herself is not unscathed and has become hard and cold, even repulsive. The years of trial have toughened her, so much so that she is no longer afraid of her husband. Having seen firsthand Dimmesdale's torment and his precarious mental state, and realizing that Chillingworth knows

Dimmesdale's secret and is tormenting him because of it, she resolves to remonstrate with her husband.

They speak to each other again, for the second time in the novel, in "**Hester and the Physician**." Chillingworth now presents a demonic appearance; he is hardly human anymore. Hester demands he stop his persecution of Dimmesdale. Contemplating his actions, Chillingworth arrives at a moment of horrified self-knowledge: He realizes he has become a monster. "Not improbably, he had never before viewed himself as he did now." Although he is not mollified and cannot forgive, he does not oppose Hester when she informs him of her firm intention to reveal his identity to Dimmesdale. They part company.

The following chapter, "**Hester and Pearl**," opens with a surprising admission of hatred on Hester's part for Chillingworth; she feels his crime in persuading her to marry him is far greater than her crime in betraying that marriage. There follows a rare moment of near intimacy between mother and daughter; Pearl asks Hester the meaning of the letter and links it explicitly to the reason Dimmesdale is always pressing his hand to his chest. Hester, however, cannot answer her daughter's question and, for the first time, lies about it, claiming she wears it "for the sake of its gold thread." Pearl's momentary warmth toward her mother fades away, but the girl presses the question and will not let it go, until Hester is provoked into hostility and threatens to silence Pearl. It is clear that this lasting secret not only stands between Hester and Pearl but is poised to grow and thrust them further and further apart.

Chapter 16, "**A Forest Walk**," describes how Hester arranges to meet with Dimmesdale by intercepting him on a return trip through the forest. The forest, in *The Scarlet Letter*, is the scene of the putative witches' sabbaths; it is the domain of the native inhabitants deemed "savages," and the place in which Chillingworth learned some of his medical secrets. Overall, the forest serves Hawthorne as a symbol for a place of license, where the constraints of the city and community may be thrown off, where sin may take place unpunished, where light and shadow are mixed. Pearl asks Hester to tell her the story of the Black Man, who is the devil as he appears at the sabbath. Mistress Hibbins has told Pearl about him. "Once in my life I met the Black Man," Hester says, "This scarlet letter is his mark!"

Sending Pearl off to play by a babbling brook (to which she bears no small resemblance), Hester withdraws to meet Dimmesdale. They encounter each other in the next chapter, "**The Pastor and His Parishioner**," both of them staring as if the other was a ghost. Dimmesdale complains he has no peace and can take no solace in the good he does with his ministry; the secret he keeps and the lie he hides strip everything else of its value. Stricken anew with the deep realization of how much her silence has cost him, Hester can bring herself to reveal her husband's identity only with great effort. Dimmesdale's features darken terribly at the news, but he no longer has the strength even to be angered. "'I might have known it!' murmured he. 'I did know it! . . . Why did I not understand?'" Hester embraces him and demands, implores his forgiveness. After a deep and silent inner struggle, Dimmesdale does so, saying "That old man's revenge has been blacker than my sin. He has violated, in cold blood, the sanctity of a human heart. Thou and I, Hester, never did so!"

It gradually becomes clear that Hester and Dimmesdale have come to a crossroads. Dimmesdale cannot bear to remain in Boston, and so Hester tells him he must return to England. Dimmesdale claims he does not possess strength enough to go—not alone. Hester answers, "Thou shalt not go alone!"

In the chapter that follows, "**A Flood of Sunshine**," the unremitting bleakness of the narrative up to this point gives way to a poignantly brief moment of peace. While no such idea has ever occurred to Dimmesdale, Hester, whose mind is not boxed in by ministerial rules and universal laws, has long been acquainted with the plan to leave. Dimmesdale hardly dares believe it possible; his leaden spirits begin to recover at once. Hester unpins the scarlet letter from her breast and throws it away; she also releases her hair from the cap that normally confined it. The life and beauty that seven years of ostracism had drained from her returns in an instant, and she calls to Pearl, who appears adorned in flowers and green twigs, like a pagan spirit.

Now Pearl must confront and understand this new turn of events, as described in **"The Child at the Brook-Side."** She is described as "the oneness of their being," the living embodiment of their union. Dimmesdale observes his daughter with feelings of trepidation and anticipation; he wants to love his daughter and be loved by her, but he understands that, in denying her as his own, he has denied her something precious. Pearl comes up to them on the other side of the brook and will not cross over, despite Hester's urgings. Frowning, Pearl points rigidly at the spot on her mother's breast where the scarlet letter should be. When Hester becomes angry and orders Pearl to cross the stream and rejoin them, which would symbolically represent Pearl accepting and becoming part of their deceits, the girl responds by becoming angry herself and shrieking. She refuses even to bring her mother the scarlet letter, insisting Hester come over to her side and pick it up. Hester replaces the letter on her bosom and gathers her hair beneath her bonnet again. Only then will Pearl recognize Hester as her mother. When assured that Dimmesdale will not go into town with them, she refuses to have anything to do with him. When he kisses her, she runs back to the brook to wash herself clean of it.

Having utterly destroyed, by the agency of Pearl, any trace of the happiness invoked by their plan, Hawthorne resumes his scrutiny of Dimmesdale in **"The Minister in a Maze."** A "questionable cruiser," bound for Bristol, is docked in Boston Harbor. Hester, in her charitable work, has become acquainted with the captain of this vessel and will be able to procure passage for the three of them easily. Even more fortuitously, the ship is not set to depart for another four days: Dimmesdale has been selected to preach the Election Sermon, the most important single function any New England minister could perform, in three days. "'At least, they shall say of me,' thought this exemplary man, 'that I leave no public duty unperformed, nor ill performed!'"

In his excitement over the prospect of escape, Dimmesdale begins to unravel mentally. Meeting a venerable deacon in the church, he finds he can barely stop himself from blaspheming in his presence; meeting an old woman who had lost her entire family, he has difficulty refraining from offering her arguments against the immortality of the soul; he is also tempted to join in the indecorous debauches of a group of sailors. Returning to his senses, he marvels at the near madness that seems poised to overwhelm him; it seems as though he has made a devil's bargain, to buy happiness at the cost of righteousness, and that the Reverend Dimmesdale who entered the forest is dead and gone, replaced by a new and wholly different man. Returning home, Dimmesdale encounters Chillingworth, and, although they exchange words in their habitual way, Chillingworth discerns at once that Dimmesdale knows his true identity. Dimmesdale dispenses with Chillingworth's medical attention, burns the sermon he had been writing, and sets to work on a new one, which he, in a state of mental exaltation, writes in the course of a single night.

Now the pace of the narrative accelerates. In "**The New England Holiday**," we have already reached the day of the sermon. The inhabitants of Boston are preparing for their rather drab festivities. As Hester surveys the scene, she notes the presence of Roger Chillingworth, deep in conversation with the captain of the Bristol-bound ship. Chillingworth withdraws, and Hester inquires of the captain, privately, what was the matter of his business with the doctor; he informs her that Chillingworth has booked passage on the same ship and is resolved to go wherever she and Dimmesdale go. Hester can see Chillingworth smiling blandly at her from across the marketplace. She may escape Puritan Boston, but his vengeance will pursue her and Dimmesdale forever, or so he wishes them to think.

In "**The Procession**," the celebration begins in earnest. Various civil and religious leaders parade through town. Dimmesdale is among their number and, while still physically debilitated, exhibits unusual energy and vigor; he also seems to be caught up in a sort of trance, noticing nothing around him. Mistress Hibbins passes by, laughingly claiming that Dimmesdale, as grand as he might appear, is one of the devil's own; no one seems to take her opinions seriously, however. In the meantime, Dimmesdale has begun to deliver his sermon with all the thrilling and sympathetic power at his command. Hester listens, rapt, but also aware of the unwelcome and judging eyes that continually fall on her and her letter. Pearl is called a "witch-baby" by one of the sailors, who gives her a message to pass on to Hester, to the effect that Chillingworth will himself place Dimmesdale on the boat, so that Hester need trouble herself about no one but Pearl. A subtle feeling of suspense permeates this chapter, as the novel's events coalesce to the conclusion.

Chapter 23 is titled "**The Revelation of the Scarlet Letter.**" The sermon reaches its triumphant end, and Dimmesdale is swept out of the church by a throng of admiring officials. "He stood, at this moment, on the very proudest eminence of superiority, to which the gifts of intellect, rich lore, prevailing eloquence, and reputation of whitest sanctity, could exalt a clergyman in New England's earliest days. . . ." The procession resumes, but now Dimmesdale appears to have lost all his force; he is so frail he can barely walk and yet pushes aside all offers of assistance. He approaches Hester and Pearl where they stand and stops before them, calling them by name. Chillingworth rushes forward with uncanny speed, trying to stop him, but Dimmesdale rebuffs him; it is not clear whether or not he has any knowledge of Chillingworth's plan to accompany them to England. Leaning on Hester, Dimmesdale climbs to the platform on which she was originally exposed, turns to the crowd, and confesses; he pulls open his shirt and shows his chest to the crowd, to its great shock and consternation. Hawthorne is somewhat coy about it, but the reader is plainly meant at least to entertain the idea that the letter *A* is there, carved into Dimmesdale's flesh. He slumps to the platform, nearly fainting, and Chillingworth is at his side, repeating "Thou hast escaped me!" Feeling his life escaping, Dimmesdale asks Pearl if she will kiss him; she does, and a spell was broken. The great scene of grief, in which the wild infant bore a part, had developed all her sympathies; and as her tears fell upon her father's cheek, they were the pledge that she would grow up amid human joy and sorrow, nor for ever do battle with the world, but be a woman in it.

It is perhaps only at this point that Hawthorne makes clear the extremity of the stakes involved in Pearl's relationship to her father. Praising God's name, Dimmesdale dies.

In the "**Conclusion**," we learn that there is considerable disagreement among the public, even among those who were there, as to how Dimmesdale came to have the letter on his chest, or if there were any such letter there at all. Chillingworth, who had lived for years with no other object than exacting revenge on Dimmesdale, rapidly declines and dies less than a year later, leaving Pearl "a very considerable amount of property, both here and in England" in his will. Evidently, Dimmesdale's death may have given him cause to reflect on his malice and attempt to make amends. Pearl and Hester return to England for a time, but eventually Hester comes back to her modest old home on the outskirts of Boston, still wearing the scarlet letter. Pearl marries into a noble family in England, and Hester is well provided for in her old age. She continues to perform good deeds in the community until her death and is buried next to Dimmesdale.

The Scarlet Letter is not a love story; none of the characters is able freely to love any of the others. It is not even entirely clear that Hester and Dimmesdale love each other; their "crime" seems to overwhelm and cancel the possibility of any feeling other than shame, excepting those rare moments in which they actually are in each other's presence. They do not pine for each other, and this subtly suggests that their relations have a purely spontaneous and natural character and therefore that their "crime" is better understood as a momentary lapse in judgment. As for the other characters, an intangible barrier of misfired sympathy separates Hester from Pearl. While Hester wants to give Pearl her love, Pearl refuses to accept it because Hester denies her daughter her father's presence and identity. Chillingworth seems entirely unable to love, his marriage to Hester a failed attempt to kindle feelings he is no longer able to feel. Love and friendship are alien to the Puritans in general, as Hawthorne depicts them.

Are Hawthorne's Puritans vicious? We understand them to be vulgar, crude, and moblike. They are unreasoning, unwilling or unable to understand, and without compassion. Do they demand draconian punishment as a compensation for all they have renounced? Do they resent others indulging in those vices they are denied? Clearly, many of the women in the community resented Hester even before her adultery; she is a "proud beauty," and their unacknowledged jealousy demands her humiliation. The men are portrayed as not reacting to Hester in so targeted or personal a way; their condemnation has a perfunctory air that in some ways makes it worse. They impose a life-altering punishment on Hester, and, while they take into account certain mitigating circumstances, they refuse to see her as a person. None of the Puritans truly engages with Hester; each deals with circumstances and appearances, not with feelings or motives, and not with spirit.

The carefully drawn portrait of this religious community was most likely intentional on Hawthorne's part: the Puritans are not evil nor especially cruel; their cruelty, their hypocrisy, their bigotry are all side effects of the ubiquitous meanness that is their principal trait. The Puritans depicted by Hawthorne are petty, small minded, and cramping; they apply a single standard to any number of diverse life experiences and events. They are superstitious, dogmatic, and provincial. This is part of *The Scarlet Letter*'s sophistication; the Puritans are not merely sinister hypocrites, ready-made villains, like the Catholic inquisitors of gothic novels. They are not evil, but they do evil, because they are blind to their own sins. Whenever they encounter something to which they are unable to apply one of their moral formulas, they condemn it out of hand and then ignore or forget about it. It does not occur to them to question their own practices and motives.

Hawthorne is sensitive to this kind of response to evil, the vehement refusal to examine it, the insistence that it be banished, taken away out of sight at once like a loathsome insect. With considerable psychological acuity, he understands that there may be some deeper reason for this rigid denial, that the rejector may be thereby exhibiting indirectly a sign that he or she has struggled in private with this very evil—that they are perhaps voicing aloud those cries they normally keep to themselves. Hawthorne does not restrict his argument to this alone, though, saying that the Puritans reject Hester only because they secretly hate the moral law that binds them. This is the case with some of the community members, but others condemn her for different reasons; there is a range of responses. Among the Puritans, conformity and a blind and unquestioning compliance prevail. Rules and codes of morality and conduct are accepted at face value with no inquiry into the reasons for such strictures or the justice with which they are applied and by whom. Christian law has both a letter and a spirit; one must not adhere so strictly to the rules that one loses sight of their original, higher purpose. Any sense of the spirit of the law, however, in an evolving or fluid moral and societal code, is lacking in the Puritan Boston of *The Scarlet Letter*.

For Hawthorne, one of the greatest possible shortcomings, and a common one in any era, is the cultish, blind conformity his Puritans exhibit; their morality is a matter of obeying rules without question. Hawthorne would argue, on the contrary, that moral action is a matter of decision, freely made in the sovereignty of an individual over his or her own fate. It is the grossest of infractions against another human being to attempt to determine his or her own fate, which is the substance of Hester's punishment. Therefore, *The Scarlet Letter* is not so much the story of a misconstrued crime that is hyperbolically punished by a bigoted community, but a story in which the punishment of a crime is vastly worse than the crime itself, which Hawthorne only implies in actuality. He is deliberately vague about this, so as not to prescribe to the reader a given moral reading or interpretation: To do so would be to fly in the face of the novel's central preoccupation with the freedom of the individual to judge matters morally in accordance with his or her own conscience.

Hester, with Hawthorne's tacit approval, defies this prescripted fate and develops her own; for it is not only wrong, but folly, to try to control the fate of another, since we are all, according to Hawthorne, inalienably independent. Chillingworth will learn the same lesson with regard to Dimmesdale. He cannot prevent his public confession: Whether or not Dimmesdale remains in Chillingworth's power is entirely up to Dimmesdale. Once he has shaken off Chillingworth's yoke, Dimmesdale cannot be captured again. Dimmesdale escapes strong censure in the unfolding of the novel because he subjects himself to his own grossly exaggerated self-punishment, an effective death sentence. While Hester is an outsider who is publically banished, and while she accepts her guilt and her punishment, she is on one side of this confrontation between society and the individual. Dimmesdale, on the other hand, physically embodies this struggle: He is both the sinning individual and representative of the moral (as opposed to the temporal) leader of the community; in a sense, he *is* the community. He is the voice of its moral code, the very code that condemns him. The confrontation between Dimmesdale the sinner and Dimmesdale the minister is played out internally, and this accounts for his paralysis and torment. It manifests itself physically in his frenzies and his weariness, much less in his impulse for self-mutilation. As a representative of the whole community, he also at times seems to embody qualities that imply the presence of barely restrained depravity, as during the walk home from the woods when he can hardly stop himself from acting devilish, shouting insults, and carousing with sailors. If he has these impulses, surely the townspeople do too.

What is the nature and import of the Puritans' hypocrisy? They certainly do not all long to perform what they condemn in action—this would be hypocritical if they all were adulterers and other various sinners and Hester was punished only because she was friendless or unlucky. Hawthorne knows better than to make things so easy. So, what is the shape and implication of their hypocrisy? It lies in the fact that they profess themselves Christians and as such are morally obligated to forgive, to accept, and to relate to those around them as human beings first and foremost, as "neighbors," and only thereafter in their particularities, as governor or beggar, man or woman, saint or sinner. These Christians, however, invert this in practice, they have made Christianity the religion of unflagging judgment, unrelenting punishment, and absolute intolerance of any human failing, even the slightest mistake. That being the case, those who have not fallen out of favor must not have made even a single mistake or committed a solitary sin; in other words, they must be perfect. This is why, in part, Hawthorne is careful to point out that Dimmesdale becomes an even more effective minister as a man with a secret sin on his conscience. This flatly contradicts the idea that the congregation is composed of perfect saints, and it makes a mockery of a society that purports unerringly to search out and punish sin detected in its ranks.

Chillingworth is different; he is not filled with moral outrage at the crime. It is instead a passionless, cold jealousy that drives him to persecute Dimmesdale, and he perseveres not to satisfy his hatred or injured pride, which would be bad enough, but merely to satisfy his vile curiosity. His vendetta becomes an experiment, at most tinged with hate; the demonic glee that he expresses from time to time is at most only lightly infused with feeling. It is not hate or jealousy that makes him demonic, but this disinterested delight in watching the moral degradation of another human being. The great irony of Chillingworth's character is that, while he in effect has Dimmesdale's soul lying exposed before him, like a specimen on a doctor's dissecting table, and exhibits expert knowledge of its every feature, his own soul is utterly invisible to him. Chillingworth does not see or understand with any degree of clarity his own compromised and declining state, that he is becoming a monster, his humanity dwindling or being willingly given away.

Critical Views

JAMIE BARLOWE ON "HESTER-PRYNNE-ISM"

The Scarlet Letter has often been taught as a moral text in high school and university classrooms in the United States, with Hester Prynne as the scarlet (white) woman/adulteress who serves as a cultural warning to girls and women and, therefore, as part of the social conditioning they internalize. Darrel Abel, in *The Moral Picturesque*, articulates the warning as he moralizes about Hester's "moral inadequacy" and "moral dereliction," saying that she "unwomaned herself and deluded herself with mistaken notions" (181, 187). Wendy Martin recontextualized this kind of warning more than twenty years ago:

> As daughters of Eve, American heroines [including Hester Prynne] are destined to lives of dependency and servitude as well as to painful and sorrowful childbirth because, like their predecessor, they have dared to disregard authority or tradition in search of wisdom and happiness; like Eve, heroines of American fiction are fallen women. (258)

Yet despite Wendy Martin's prominence in feminist studies, her challenging critique has had almost no effect on mainstream scholarship on *The Scarlet Letter*. Similarly, such critiques by other women have had little measurable or lasting impact on the culture's or the academy's attitudes about women.

In fact, Hester-Prynne-ism has taken all kinds of bizarre and moralizing cultural twists and turns—for example, in 1991, in Iowa: "Pointing to Hester Prynne's badge of shame as a model for their recommendation, some officials . . . hoped to curb drunken driving by requiring offenders to display car tags labelling themselves as having been guilty of DUI charges" (*NHR* 26; see also Schell, "Three-Time Loser DUIs get a Scarlet Letter 'Z'"). In an article entitled "Handing Out Scarlet Letters," *Time* magazine reports that partners seeking divorces are relying on outdated anti-adultery laws that primarily privilege men (see A. Sachs).

There is even a chapter by Peter French in a book on business ethics, called "The Hester-Prynne Sanction." In *Computerworld* Thornton May describes how electronic commerce approaches the Internet through four literary categories, one of which is the scarlet letter, and in *Broadcasting and Cable* Joe Flint argues that a ratings system for violent television shows "could be an economic scarlet letter" (33; see also Gordon, *The Scarlet Woman of Wall Street*, and McCormack on the 1990 elections). The scarlet A shows up as well in an article by Harry Hadd in *Steroids*: "The Scarlet Letter: Reichstein's Substance S"; in a *Policy Review* essay, "A Farmer's Scarlet Letter: Four Generations of Middle-Class Welfare Is Enough," by Blake Hurst; and in an essay in the book *Misdiagnosis: Woman as a Disease*, published by the People's Medical Society, entitled "Norplant: The 'Scarlet Letter' of Birth Control" by June Adinah. Hester's A has also been modernized to symbolize AIDS—for example, in *Computer/ Law Journal* as "The Scarlet Letter 'A': AIDS in a Computer Society" (van Dam)—or, to designate modern women who, "as Hester Prynne before them, are 'challenging the mores set down for them by contemporary society . . . [and have been] similarly stigmatized, branded with the scarlet A, for Autocratic, Aggressive, Authoritarian, Arrogant'" (S. Easton 740). In *Time*, the A is designated as "Today's Scarlet Letter: Herpes" (see also Osborne), and Brenda Daly uses the scarlet letter to discuss incest survival and incest narratives (155–88).

Newsweek describes Reggie Jackson as "the Hester Prynne of sluggers . . . with a scarlet dollar sign on his chest" (*NHSN* 8), and the scarlet letter is used in *Sports Illustrated* as a reference to Ohio State and Penn State football rankings (see Layden). In a 1989 article in the *Houston Post* the scarlet letter refers to an affair between baseballer Wade Boggs and Margo Adams (Robertson). In an interview question on the NBC *Nightly News* the A is mentioned when the registration of sex offenders was likened to an "unfair scarlet letter" (July 3, 1995; see also Earl Hubbard, "Child Sex Offender Registration Laws";

Suffolk University Law School, "Ex Post Facto Analysis of Sex Offender Registration Statutes: Branding Criminals with a Scarlet Letter"; Kabat, "Scarlet Letter Sex Offender Databases and Community Notification"; Kimball, "A Modern Day Arthur Dimmesdale: Public Notification When Sex Offenders Are Released into the Community").

Recently, a newspaper article reported that "Nathaniel Hawthorne's Hester Prynne had to wear a single scarlet letter to identify herself as an adulteress. A judge in Illinois went much further . . . ordering 48 letters, each 8 inches high, on a sign on a felon's property . . . WARNING A VIOLENT FELON LIVES HERE. TRAVEL AT YOUR OWN RISK." The Illinois Supreme Court, however, decided that such "humiliation is unnecessary and unfair . . . and ordered the sign taken down" ("Scarlet letters in Illinois"; see also Feldman, "The 'Scarlet Letter Laws' of the 1990s" and Reske, "Scarlet Letter Sentences"). This judgment exceeds even that of Hawthorne, who read about such punishments in Joseph B. Felt's 1827 *The Annals of Salem*, which explained: "[I]n 1694, a law was passed requiring adulterers to wear a two-inch-high capital A, colored to stand out against the background of the wearer's clothes" (*TSL: Case Studies* 12; see also Hawthorne, "The Custom-House" 41). By 1782, the use of the scarlet letter for adulterers was discontinued in New England (Davidson and Wagner-Martin 950).

Hester-Prynne-ism shows up even in the military. The first woman bomber pilot, Lt. Kelly Flinn, was generally (not honorably) discharged in 1997 by the Air Force for the admitted charges of adultery and lying. Wire services reported as follows: "Lieutenant Flinn, 26, who is single, was charged with committing adultery with a married man. Her allies assailed the military for branding her with a scarlet letter for allegedly committing an act that many male officers have done with impunity" ("Embattled Female Pilot"). The *New Yorker* also picks up on the connection between the treatment of Flinn and Hawthorne's romance:

> There is nothing funny about the contretemps for
> Lieutenant Flinn; she is no longer in danger of doing time

in a military prison, but her pioneering military career has been ruined, and her less than honorable discharge is a stigma. The rest of us, though, can be forgiven for having found entertainment in this unexpected Pentagon production of "The Scarlet Letter" and in the enduring ridiculousness of our antiquated and unenforceable sex laws. (Angell 4)

Another instance of a reference to the scarlet A and Lt. Flinn occurs in a May 29, 1997 newspaper cartoon in which a line of formidable-looking Air Force officers are headed by one who holds a branding iron with a red-hot A; he says, "Lieut. Flinn, Step Forward." In the corner of the cartoon, a little bird says, "They want you to take it like a man" (see also Barto, "The Scarlet Letter and the Military Justice System"; S. Chase, "The Woman Who Fell to Earth"). Even more recently, William Ginsberg, the former attorney for Monica Lewinsky, stated on CNN on January 25, 1998 that Lewinsky may have to wear "the scarlet letter of indictment for the rest of her life."

Literarily, John Updike's book *S* "turns to Sarah Worth, a modern version of Hester Prynne. . . . Instead of having a way with a needle Sarah has a way with a pen or tape recorder— after all she is a woman of the 1980's" (*NHR* 26; see also Updike's *Roger's Version*). Grace Jones argues convincingly that another Sarah, John Fowles's Sarah Woodruff in the *French Lieutenant's Woman*, "is a Victorian Hester . . . Hester's true child . . . [and] proof of how slow is the evolutionary process Hester envisioned" (78, 71). Christopher Bigsby's novel, *Hester: A Romance* (1994), is a prequel to *The Scarlet Letter*, narrating the time from Hester's birth, as herself a "bastard" child, to her death; Bigsby claims to have written the novel because, "repeating Dimmesdale's sin," he "fell in love with" Prynne (188). Charles Larson's novel, *Arthur Dimmesdale* (1983), opens after Hester Prynne's admission to Dimmesdale that she is pregnant and ends as Pearl kisses him and he dies. The protagonist of Bharati Mukherjee's novel, *The Holder of the World* (1993), Beigh Masters, discovers her ancestor Hannah Easton, who was Hester Prynne. Born in Salem, and later marrying an Englishman, Hannah moves to India, where she becomes the mistress of a Raja. Then, pregnant by him, she returns to Salem. (See also Kathy Acker's *Blood and Guts in High School*.)

From the 1870s on, dramatic productions have refocused attention on Prynne's scarlet A; for example, Joseph Hatton's *The Scarlet Letter, or Hester Prynne* (1870), Emile de Najac's five-act tragedy *The Scarlet Letter* (1876), James Edgar Smith's *The Scarlet Stigma* (1899), Phyllis Nagy's adaptation of *The Scarlet Letter for the American Theatre* (1995), and the opera based on *The Scarlet Letter* (Lathrop and Damrosch 1896). Mysteries, both dramatic and literary, have also made use of Prynne's symbolic A, as it designates evil and adultery or threatens disruption—for example, in *The Perfect Crime*, now in its eighth year of off-Broadway production, in Ellery Queen's *Scarlet Letters*, and in a recent detective novel by Julie Smith, *The Axeman's Jazz* (see also Maron, Steinberg). In *Primal Fear*, a film released in 1996, the killing of a Catholic bishop is underscored with references to *The Scarlet Letter*. The killer, in fact, leaves an underlined section of the text as a clue to his motivation for the slaying (see also Diehl).

Paradoxically, the mainstream body of scholarship on *The Scarlet Letter* has functioned as both a moralizing warning and radical model to women who choose not to act fully in terms of their social conditioning—for example, women in an academy where male critics and scholars admire the duplicitous radical subversion of men like Nathaniel Hawthorne and hold up as a model his male fantasy of a radical, subversive woman, Hester Prynne, who can be reread as profoundly (hetero)sexualized and objectified, as one who "stands by her man," and as one who finally self-punishes.[6] As Sacvan Bercovitch has claimed, Hester finds "conversion to the letter" at the end of the text (*Office* 3). Or, as Millicent Bell put it more than thirty years ago, Hester, like other of Hawthorne's "most memorable female characters" (Beatrice, Zenobia, Miriam, and Drowne's mysterious model), "suggests experience . . . knowledge . . . [and] sin, the moral cost of experience and knowledge, which is the artist's [and the critic's] peril" (*Hawthorne's View* 133).

Note

6. Many women have argued that Hester Prynne's return to Boston at the end of the text, her resumption of the wearing of the scarlet A, and her recognition that she is not "fit" to be the spokeswoman of change for women is evidence of Hawthorne's nonradical relationship to his character and to feminist issues of his time. Many have more generally critiqued Prynne as a female representation, taking her creator to task for his male fantasizing about a strong woman whom he will later subdue completely. See chapter 4.

PATRICIA CRAIN DISCUSSES ALLEGORY, ADULTERY, AND ALPHABETIZATION

In "The Custom-House" the A is "twisted" around the "small roll of dingy paper" that contains "a reasonably complete explanation of the whole affair" (32). Like the microcosmic A in an alphabet book, suggesting the macrocosm of A-words, the scarlet letter both is contained by and contains the narrative of *The Scarlet Letter*. This synecdochic relation of the narrative to its origin in the alphabetic character lays the groundwork for Hawthorne's allegorical mode in the novel. As the ur-letter, the A unfolds to produce writing, and it subjects all within its purview to the strictures of written or printed discourse. It is in this active sense rather than in any set of one-to-one correspondences that *The Scarlet Letter* may be read as an allegory of alphabetization. The binding of the alphabetical character to the bodies of Hester, Pearl, and Arthur requires varying degrees of bodily conformation or distortion and the infliction of various kinds and degrees of pain; this binding and conformation constitutes their alphabetization.

"Allegory," as Angus Fletcher describes its etymology, derives from "*allos + agoreuein (other + speak openly, speak in the assembly or market). Agoreuein* connotes public, open declarative speech. This sense is inverted by the prefix *allos*" (2). *Allos*, "other," modifies the radical for speaking publicly (in the *agora*, the forum or marketplace) in "allegory." If allegory describes the translating efforts of the author as well as the interpretive efforts of the reader, what translates the characters in *The Scarlet Letter* from one state or status to another is adultery. The words share an etymological bond. "Adultery" is rooted in an unadulterated "other"; according to Partridge (*Origins*), the sense of the Latin *adulteādre* is *adalterāre*, literally, "to alter." If allegory means to *speak* "other," adultery means to *be* other. When the letter translates Hester's body into a public space, she has become "the other" in the marketplace, there to be read and interpreted. Allegory, adultery, and alphabetization all require a transformation from one state or status to another; in each case, the realms of official conduct and private experience exist in tension with each other, or come into open conflict.

The liminality inherent in these three terms is captured in the opening chapter of the novel, "The Prison-Door." The narrative emerges from the customhouse, both figuratively, since there the narrator finds the A and the bare bones of his story, and literally, as "The Custom-House" introduces the novel. The customhouse opens onto a world of commerce with faraway places, but it is also, as the house of custom, the site of cultural rituals. As the novel opens, however, the venue has shifted from "The Custom-House" to "The Prison-Door." In a metonymic reduction, the house distills down to a door, and all its customs to the disciplines of the prison.

Hawthorne arrays a catalog of ill-lettered figures, in nearly primer-like alphabetical order, who might issue from the prison into the marketplace in chapter 2: "bond-servant," "child," "heterodox religionist," "Indian," "witch" (49). In the place of these malefactors, Hester emerges. The bloodthirsty matrons in the crowd want to strip Hester (54), brand her on the forehead, kill her (51). The A deflects, suppresses, and compresses within itself these radical solutions. The A's first task is to contain, and eventually dissipate, the violent desires of the crowd. The only discipline Hester will receive is the discipline of the alphabet. The A thus substitutes for fatal punishment; it "stands for," stands in the place of, death. At the same time, by deferring Hester's death the A gives birth to the narrative. The first power of the A, then, to give life, is aligned with Hester's maternity. Hester's adultery would never have been discovered if not for her pregnancy. If her fertility has engendered the A, the A returns the favor, extending Hester's life.

Hester begins as a Bellerophon figure, bearing a written sign, like his, and like his meant to discipline her for illicit love.[20] Through epic endurance Hester, like Bellerophon, outstrips her punishers and her punishment. Like Bellerophon, Hester undergoes heroic struggles and wanders alone like him, whom Homer describes as "devouring his own soul, and shunning the paths of men" (6:200–203). Like him, Hester is "banished and as much alone as if she inhabited another sphere, or communicated with the common nature by other organs and senses than the rest of human kind" (84). Bellerophon carries his "baneful tokens" from the writer to the reader, remaining, himself, outside the realm of text, though influenced by it. But Hester wears her A with a difference because she is able to read her own sign.

"Tall," a woman "on a large scale," with "abundant hair . . . a marked brow and deep black eyes," Hester has "impressiveness" and "a certain state and dignity" (53). . . . Hester is large as a reminder of her recent pregnancy, and she is large to distinguish her from woman in the nineteenth century. She is large to provide a canvas for the A; she is a sculpture, a painting by Raphael, a picture in an emblem book: Grammatica, for example. She is large, like a monument, to hold the gaze of the audience; she is large because she has to remain visible from afar. She is large so that Hawthorne, and the reader, can be small.

Moreover, Hester is large because the A has transformed her into a public space. The modern form of capital letters originates in letters incised in stone; the capital letter is inherently monumental.[21] . . .

Hester is "transfigured" (53) by the fateful letter on her bosom: "It had the effect of a spell, taking her out of the ordinary relations with humanity, and inclosing her in a sphere by herself" (54). The A submits Hester to a rite of transition, but her liminality dilates for the length of her life.[23] The isolated letter, as if by contagion, isolates Hester. But isolation is an effect, too, of silent, solitary reading. As though undergoing a ritual process, Hester "felt or fancied, then, that the scarlet letter had endowed her with a new sense." The A "gave her a sympathetic knowledge of the hidden sin in other hearts" (86). Like McLuhan's "extensions of man," the A allows Hester to exceed the limits of her body by giving her the power to read people as texts, to enter into them without their knowledge. Not only does Hester read others, but she must patiently endure being read by them. "Both men and women, who had been familiarly acquainted with Hester Prynne, were now impressed as if they beheld her for the first time" (53). The A's melding to Hester defamiliarizes her and at the same time gives her the power to "impress" or imprint, as if the A were a piece of type and the crowd Hester's blank page. But more often, Hester herself is the page: Chillingworth sees her becoming "a living sermon against sin, until the ignominious letter be engraved upon her tombstone" (63). At church, "it was often her mishap to find herself the text of the discourse" (85) as she is presented as an allegory for the congregation. . . .

Hawthorne treats Hester and Pearl as letter-men, for they are precisely in the predicament of having a relative and composite meaning that is outside them. More than Hester, who is painfully initiated into the alphabetical world, Pearl is the product of alphabetization as much as the progeny of Hester and Arthur, as though she were the offspring rather of Grammatica and Rhetorica. The ultimate alphabetized child, Pearl is like an isolated image in an alphabet book. . . .

Like the child-man Hawthorne finding the letter in the customhouse, baby Pearl is full of desire for the mother's A: "Putting up her little hand, she grasped at it, smiling, not doubtfully, but with a decided gleam that gave her face the look of a much older child" (96). And as in "The Custom-House," the narrator stumbles over his language, opening gaps in the flow of the text, gaps that open onto a preliterate orality, in an attempt to describe the scene of Pearl's discovery of language. Rather than finding her mirror in the mother's face, Pearl finds it in the A. Rather than an "embryo smile" in mirror-response, Pearl gives "a decided gleam that gave her face the look of a much older child." "Gleam" is associated in *The Scarlet Letter* with the letter: "It was whispered, by those who peered after her, that the scarlet letter threw a lurid gleam along the dark passage-way of the interior" (69). Pearl "imprints," as naturalists say of animal relations, not, as is the usual case, on her mother, but on the A.

In essence, Pearl reads before she speaks; she literally rather than figuratively takes in the alphabet with mother's milk. By the age of three, without books, Pearl knows the contents of the Westminster Catechism and *The New England Primer* (112). Having so early imbibed the letter, Pearl forms an indissoluble unit with the A. More even than Hester, Pearl has become a sign, "the scarlet letter endowed with life, only capable of being loved" (113). Hester and Pearl have so conformed to the written sign that they have no existence outside or beyond it.

Notes

20. The story of Bellerophon is the only reference to writing in Homer (*Iliad* 6:160ff.). The beautiful and brave Bellerophon snubs the seducing Anteia, wife of Proitos, Argive king. In revenge, Anteia accuses Bellerophon of attempted rape, whereupon Proitos banishes him to Lycia, with "baneful tokens, graving in a folded tablet many signs and deadly, and bade him show these to his own wife's father, that he might be slain." Roy Harris suggests that in this story "writing stands between the individual and an understanding of his own fate" (16). See also Stroud for the context of the Bellerophon story. Hawthorne picks up the Bellerophon tale at a later point in *The Wonder Tales*, where the hero tames Pegasus and vanquishes the chimaera.

21. See Tschichold, 20: "The upper and lower case letters received their present form in the Renaissance. The serifs of the capitals, or upper case letters, were adapted to those of the lower case alphabet. The capitals are based on an incised or chiseled letter; the lower case characters are based on a pen-written calligraphic form."

23. See van Gennep, esp. 120–121, and 190–192.

DAVID S. REYNOLDS ON
HAWTHORNE'S REVISION OF HISTORY

Hawthorne's *The Scarlet Letter* (1850) has long been regarded as one of America's classic historical novels. . . .

In the discussion of historical context, what has been largely disregarded is the degree to which Hawthorne determinedly reshaped the Puritan past in order to satisfy the tastes of his own contemporary readership in nineteenth-century America. The relationship between *The Scarlet Letter* and Puritan history is analogous to that between the R-rated 1995 movie version of the novel and the novel itself. Just as the director Roland Joffe catered to moviegoers by sensationalizing Hawthorne's narrative, . . . so Hawthorne sensationalized Puritanism by introducing fictional elements he knew were attractive to novel readers in the 1840s.

Contrary to popular belief, Hawthorne in *The Scarlet Letter* was not particularly original in his choice of characters or themes. A reason the novel became one of his most popular works was that the antebellum public felt comfortable with a fictional expose of hidden corruption involving a hypocritical preacher, a fallen woman, an illegitimate child, and a vindictive relative. By the late 1840s such depraved characters were stock figures in American fiction. . . .

Secret sexual escapades among preachers were such common topics in sensational fiction that one hostile reviewer, Arthur Cleveland Coxe, declared that Hawthorne's tale of the "nauseous amour of a Puritan pastor" was a book "made for the market" like many popular seamy works, "because," Coxe explained, "a running undertide of filth has become as requisite to a romance, as death in the fifth act of a tragedy." The antebellum public had a special interest in sensational sex scandals involving clergymen. Stories of so-called reverend rakes ensured a good sale for newspapers and crime pamphlets, while the more traditional virtuous preacher was considered too dull to sell copy. . . .

Hawthorne's Arthur Dimmesdale, then, had many forerunners in popular newspapers. He had even more in popular novels, in which the reverend rake was typically portrayed as a manipulative clergyman with an overactive sex drive. By the 1840s, the reverend rake had become so common a figure in popular fiction that Hawthorne could not overlook it in his search for a main male character for *The Scarlet Letter*. . . .

Dimmesdale is not the only character in *The Scarlet Letter* with predecessors in antebellum culture. Another is Hester Prynne, who can be viewed as a composite of female heroines in popular fiction. Hawthorne, a close reader of popular newspapers, may have seen in the *Salem Gazette* for January 29, 1833, a story called "The Magdalene," which recounts a squalid life of sin followed by her penitence (much like Hester Prynne's) while living in an isolated cottage and doing charity work for a nearby village. But Hester is not only the sympathetically portrayed fallen woman. She is also the struggling working woman who plies her needle as a seamstress; the feminist criminal bound in an "iron link of mutual crime" with a relatively feeble man; and the sensual woman who, in Hawthorne's words, has "a rich, voluptuous, Oriental characteristic" and who whispers to her lover, "What we did had a consecration of its own." She is the feminist exemplar who broods privately over women's wrongs and dreams of a revolution in relations between the sexes. All these iconoclastic female character types had been widely disseminated in subversive popular literature of the day. Hawthorne's innovation was to combine these rebellious traits in a heroine who also exhibits more conventional qualities as well. Like the heroines of the "scribbling women" Hawthorne aspersed (and half-envied for their popularity), Hester elicits from others "the reverence due to an angel," and one of the meanings associated with her letter is "Angel." Along with her angelic quality goes a practical ability to help others as a charity worker and an adviser.

In fashioning his main characters, therefore, Hawthorne borrowed extensively from popular culture. But he not only adopted popular character types; he determinedly transformed them, and his chief transforming agent was Puritanism. As much as he disliked the severity of the Puritans, he admired their moral seriousness, which he believed had been lost over time. Several times in the novel he pauses to indict what he sees as the crassness of nineteenth-century sensationalism. He underscores the soberness of Puritan punishment of sin by writing that "a penalty, which, in our days, would infer a degree of mocking infamy and ridicule, might then be invested with almost as stern a dignity as the punishment of death itself." He writes that the Puritans "had none of the heartlessness of another social state, which would find only a theme for jest in an exhibition like the present." He stresses that the Puritans valued "stability and dignity of character a great deal more" than contemporary Americans, and they possessed "the quality of reverence, which, in their descendants, if it survive at all, exists in smaller proportion, and with vastly diminished force."

Throughout the novel, Hawthorne treats earnestly topics that in popular sensational literature had become matters of mechanical prurience and shallow irreverence. True, he makes use of stock situations—a clergyman adulterously involved with a young woman; angry revenge against the lovers by the woman's cuckolded husband; gleeful reveling in sin by devilish side characters; and references to "mysterious" pseudosciences like alchemy and mesmerism. But because he allows such sensational images to resonate within a Puritan culture described with sympathy and seriousness, they never become gratuitous or perverse. Were Arthur Dimmesdale merely a reverend rake, he would be like the coarse, lip-smacking ministers of popular fiction. Because he is both a reverend rake and a devout Puritan Calvinist, he is sincerely tormented and explosively ironic. He tells Hester, "Were I an atheist,—a man devoid of conscience,—a wretch with coarse and brutal instincts,—I might have found peace, long ere now." He possesses both the profound convictions of the soul-searching Puritan and the lawless passions of the reverend rake. Hester, likewise, is a powerfully mixed character who is at once the rebellious modern woman and the self-lacerating Puritan. Because she brings Puritan soberness to her sin, she is inwardly tormented in a way that no popular heroine is.

Even the demonic Roger Chillingworth, an amalgam of the vindictive cuckold and evil pseudoscientist, has a retributive function absent from similar devil figures in popular fiction. His sadistic revenge leads finally to Dimmesdale's public confession of sin. As for little Pearl, she remains the anarchic, uncontrolled child (like the lawless children in pulp novels) as long as her parents remain within the amoral value system of nineteenth-century sensationalism: that is, as long as Dimmesdale remains a hypocrite cloaking his sin while Hester brandishes her sin without truly confronting it. Pearl becomes a moral, respectable person only when her parents honestly expose their sin—when Hawthorne leaves the realm of nineteenth-century sensationalism and recaptures the retributive world of Puritan Calvinism.

As important as the resonance gained from Puritanism is the control gained through structure and symbol. Whereas popular novelists like George Lippard and George Thompson burst linear plot patterns with their fervid irrationalism, Hawthorne arranges popular sensational images with almost mathematical care. The three gallows scenes, the seven-year time gap between the opening and middle sections, the studied alternation between public and private scenes, the balanced phrasing of the sentences: all of these stylistic elements have almost moral meaning for a writer who hated the disorganization of modern sensational texts. The relationships between the main characters are characterized by a profound interconnectedness that ranges from neurotic symbiosis to sadistic vampirism. Within the structure of the novel, none of the characters can exist without the others. Allegory and history also serve as important controlling devices. Although no single allegorical meaning can be assigned to the scarlet letter or other symbols, the very capacity of the letter and other allegorical elements to radiate meaning, the very suggestiveness of these elements, is an assertion of value when contrasted with the flat, directionless quality of sensational texts. The careful apportionment of nineteenth-century sensational images in a fully developed seventeenth-century New England setting is Hawthorne's highest achievement.

Simultaneously enlivening Puritanism and enriching sensationalism, Hawthorne created a resonant myth that itself has become a cornerstone of American cultural history.

HAL BLYTHE AND CHARLIE SWEET
EXAMINE HAWTHORNE'S DATING ERRORS

Nathaniel Hawthorne, like Homer, occasionally nods. In "The Minister's Black Veil," for instance, Hawthorne describes Elizabeth's inquiring as to what Hooper's veil conceals "[a]t the minister's first visit" (292). On receiving an unsatisfactory answer, Elizabeth "withdrew her arm from his grasp, and slowly departed, pausing at the door" (294). Because people rarely leave their own home when dissatisfied with a visitor, readers must conclude that Hawthorne's attention momentarily faltered here.

Another "error" appears in *The Scarlet Letter*. In "The Custom House," Hawthorne relates how he discovers "several foolscap sheets" (25) written by a predecessor, Mr. Surveyor Pue, about Hester Prynne. These six sheets supposedly offer two types of accounts about Hester: "Aged persons, alive in the time of Mr. Surveyor Pue, and from whose oral testimony he had made up his narrative, remembered her, in their youth" (25) and those who "had heard the tale from contemporary witnesses" (175).

A dating problem arises with the first group. Critics concur that historical documents place the events in *The Scarlet Letter* as starting in 1642 and ending in 1649, despite Hawthorne's claiming in paragraph two that the events occurred approximately "fifteen or twenty years" (35) after the settling of Salem in 1630. Evidently Hawthorne was not extremely concerned with absolute accuracy in dating historical events. But the problem worsens. Jonathan Pue was appointed Surveyor of Customs at Salem in 1752, and he died in 1760; in fact, Hawthorne alludes to having noticed the obituary in Joseph Felt's *The Annals of Salem, From Its First Settlement*, 1827. The problem can be simply stated: how could people alive during Hester's time still be living years later for Surveyor Pue to record their oral testimony? Hawthorne tries unsuccessfully to explain the age gap by noting that when they met Hester, she was "a very old, but not decrepit woman" (25). Let us be more exact. According to John Demos, a twenty-year-old woman who had survived childbirth could expect to live to about 62 (192). Are we to believe that these people saw Hester in their youth, perhaps around the year 1680 when Hester would have most probably been 58—very "old" but not "decrepit"? By 1727 these witnesses would have been 62 and with a normal life expectancy would have died; their deaths would have occurred more than 25 years before Pue began conducting his interviews.

Statistically, one aged person might be possible, but several? The romance tradition in which Hawthorne wrote certainly did not demand absolute fidelity to detail and even privileged possibility over probability, but why would Hawthorne go to so much trouble to establish the reality of the "found" manuscript convention, drop in real dates (e.g. the death of Governor Bellingham), and then undercut his story with suspect dating? If he wanted actual eyewitness testimony, couldn't he have used an earlier Surveyor, Measurer, or some other public authority?

One possible objection to the dating problem might be that Jonathan Pue conducted his interviews before becoming Surveyor. Hawthorne, however, concludes that Pue "being little molested . . . with business pertaining to his office—seems to have devoted some of his leisure hours to researches as a local antiquarian, and the inquisitions of a similar nature" (24). Moreover, Hawthorne describes finding the foolscap sheets at the Custom House, Pue's place of work, not at his home (where they could have been written any time). Table 1 depicts the events' probable timeline.

Ultimately, we must conclude that Hawthorne erred with his dating, undercutting his own extensive attempt to establish the reality of his characters and their lives.

Hawthorne's Timeline in *The Scarlet Letter*

Date	Action	Age
1642	Pearl is 3 months old	Hester: about 20[a]
1647	Pearl is 7 years old	Hester: about 27
1680	Witnesses see Hester as "old" but not "decrepit"	Hester: about 58; witnesses about 15 (to remember her)

1684	Hester dies	Hester: about 62 (normal life span)
1727	Witnesses die	Witnesses: about 62 (normal life span)
1752	Surveyor Pue takes office and begins interviews	

[a] Although Hawthorne reveals Pearl's age, he never notes that of Hester, so at the time of her first appearance, readers must make an educated guess about her age.

Works Cited

Demos, John. *A Little Commonwealth: Family Life in Plymouth Colony*. New York: Oxford UP, 1970.

Hawthorne, Nathaniel. "The Minister's Black Veil." *Great Short Works of Hawthorne*. Ed. Frederick Crews. New York: Harper, 1967. 285–99.

————. *The Scarlet Letter*. 3rd ed. New York: Norton, 1988.

Monika M. Elbert Considers Hester's *A*

Nathaniel Hawthorne's most famous novel, *The Scarlet Letter*, presents the modern reader with Hester Prynne, a Puritan woman living in the late seventeenth century, created from the perspective of a nineteenth-century New England writer. Although ostensibly about the Puritan way of life, the novel sheds even more light on changing gender roles in the nineteenth century. Women were traditionally supposed to take care of the home and hearth and not venture into men's world of business or public activity. Within the parameters of the "Cult of True Womanhood," middle-class women were relegated to the role of good housewife and mother in their separate domestic sphere. At first glance, Hester Prynne is certainly not the type of woman who would have been held up as a model of True Womanhood. Married to another, she has an illegitimate child, and then sets up a home of her own—without a husband by her side, as a single mother. Hawthorne has the good sense not to kill off his adulteress, a first in Anglo-American literature. Neither does he create Hester as some weak damsel in distress who needs a husband or father to guide and support her; rather, she is self-reliant, creative, and passionate.

Read within the cultural context of nineteenth-century feminism, Hester's character takes on an interesting, if enigmatic, dimension. Most likely influenced by such events as the Seneca Falls Convention (1848) and the Married Women's Property Acts, Hawthorne creates a strong female protagonist, one whom he admires but also fears on some level. She shares the same New England Transcendentalist qualities, which Emerson extolled in his famous essay, "Self-Reliance" (1841), and which Margaret Fuller apparently rewrites for a female audience in her equally famous but longer work, *Woman in the Nineteenth Century* (1845). Although initially, the townspeople's fear of Hester seems to be of her blatant sexuality, by the end of the narrative Hester appears to have been tamed, at least superficially, so that she is rendered more and more passionless, marble-like, and statue-like. However, her potential threat to the community is more evident as she becomes increasingly introspective and intellectual. In "Another View of Hester," we hear that she

> assumed a freedom of speculation, then common enough on the other side of the Atlantic, but which our forefathers, had they known of it, would have held to be a deadlier crime than that stigmatized by the scarlet letter. (133)

Hawthorne has not, then, actually tamed or domesticated his Hester; instead, she grows from being excessively passionate to being serious and intellectual, no mere feat for a nineteenth-century woman.

In essence, Hawthorne celebrates (and Hester epitomizes) not just Woman Feeling, but Woman Thinking. Not merely a mother to her own child, Hester eventually becomes the angel of the household ministering to dying parishioners as well as nurturing lovesick girls. Herself having once been impassioned and lovesick, she excels as a counselor. This book celebrates feminine intelligence, creativity, compassion, while it downplays, to Hawthorne's (and Hester's) credit, the popular and sentimental image of woman as dependent, or even worse, as victim of her romantic fantasies.

Young readers, in particular, might be confused about Hester's source of power. Is she attractive because of her stunning beauty, her sexuality, her artistry, or her intelligence? If she does seem empowered (today we admire all those qualities), what qualities would the reader feel most compelling, most important for Hester not to sacrifice to public opinion? If society is superficial, judgmental, and oppressive, how can one live within its parameters and follow its dictates? Are actions based on principle or on honesty almost always construed as simply wayward? The message may be a bit frightening, as a total departure from the norm could lead to ostracism and alienation. It is more important to delve into one's own being to find one's hidden strengths and intelligence, a psychic space within (metaphorically, Hester's isolated cottage), as Hester does, than to create a new Eden (Boston as the "City upon a Hill"), based on time-worn traditions, as the judgmental Puritans do. Hester does not pander to patriarchal authority figures to please a hypocritical or shallow crowd. Readers who are used to conforming might respond with awe to Hester's courage and individualism. Others may be interested in comparing their own acts of rebelliousness—against their parents, teachers, and their community's expectations—to Hester's.

Most feminist critics analyze the process whereby Hester subverts the laws of patriarchy and lives according to a law of her own. She transforms the original meaning of the letter "A" (adultery) so that the judgmental community comes to see her stigmatized letter as a badge of honor: people assert that "it meant Able; so strong was Hester Prynne, with a woman's strength" (131). But Hester does not accept the community's new interpretation. After many years, when the town fathers ask her to remove the "letter" and forget the past, Hester refuses. As an artist creating embroidered beauty, Hester has infused the letter as well as her existence with her own meaning. The Puritan community, who initially tried to hush her, is now hushed. Various critics have interpreted her silence (her adamant refusal to name the father of her child; her vow of secrecy to Chillingworth not to identify his relation to her) as both empowering (she thwarts the Governor and other patriarchs from learning her secret) and disempowering (she feels threatened by Chillingworth's obvious and Dimmesdale's veiled attempts to hush her). Yet silence, in Hester's case, offers a type of passive resistance to male probing; thus, her injunction to Dimmesdale at the Governor's Mansion, "Speak thou for me" (98), ultimately forces him to confront his own demons rather than to project them onto her. One might finally ask whether Hester's voicelessness or Dimmesdale's voice has more presence.

Perhaps the most disheartening quality about *The Scarlet Letter* is the conclusive, cynical view of women in which the narrator calls for some ideal vision of Womanhood so as to redeem mankind from Hester's sin: "The angel and apostle of the coming revelation must be a woman, indeed, but lofty, pure, and beautiful, and wise, moreover, not through dusky grief, but the ethereal medium of joy" (201). With this apocalyptic vision in mind, readers might wonder if placing woman on a pedestal, demanding perfection and purity, oppresses all women who could be easily stigmatized with variations of the letter "A."

SHARI BENSTOCK ON THE MOTHER-CHILD RELATIONSHIP IN THE NOVEL

Before the authorities in the governor's hall, Hester declares that Dimmesdale has sympathies that other men lack, ascribing to him knowledge of maternal matters: "thou knowest what is in my heart, and what are a mother's rights, and how much the stronger they are, when that mother has but her child and the scarlet letter" (p. 98). Her claim is that maternal ties and mother rights are stronger in the absence of the father, and she charges Dimmesdale to "look to it," that is, to see to it that she not lose her child. Although Dimmesdale's physical weakness feminizes him (he seems hardly able to support the secret phallic signifier he is supposed to bear), he argues forcefully for her in his "sweet, tremulous, but powerful" voice (p. 98). . . . The Puritan code demands that she relinquish her femininity as the price of survival; she assumes a serenity and calm that appear as "marble coldness" (p. 134). The scarlet letter, whose rich embroidery in other circumstances might be read as a sign of feminine adornment, is here the sign that Hester has forfeited her place in the normal exchange of women among men, where fathers hand daughters to husbands. The letter is Hester's "passport into regions where other women dared not tread" (p. 158).

Hester's "lost" sexual nature is transferred to her daughter, whose passionate temperament apparently knows no repression. Indeed, Pearl appears to harbor secret knowledge associated with the scarlet letter, knowledge that Hester both fears and tries to discover in her daughter's regard. . . . Hester tries through her needlework "to create an analogy between the object of her affection [Pearl], and the emblem of her guilt and torture [the letter]" (p. 90). Mother and daughter reflect each other and read each other as signs: Hester searches for evidence of an "original sin," the sin that the mother confers on the daughter through the circumstances of her conception; Pearl searches for the meaning of the scarlet letter, which she sees as the key to her mother's identity and the source of her own origins. In response to Pearl's insistent questions, Hester claims that she wears the scarlet letter "for the sake of its gold thread" (p. 145). This enigmatic response, which the child does not accept, hints that the *A* is worn for adornment and that the gold embroidery, not the letter, carries meaning. When Hester flings the letter aside in the scene by the brook, Pearl cannot recognize her *as mother* and refuses her insistent demands for recognition. By this time the effects of the scarlet letter are already lodged within the daughter's heart. Hester has succeeded in turning her daughter into a symbol, an image of the mother's (suppressed) sexual nature, by dressing her in the crimson and gold colors of the letter. . . .

The relationship of mother to child in *The Scarlet Letter* has been overlooked by traditional critics whose interpretations of the text center on the absent figure of the father and the question of paternity. However, early in the text this relationship is invoked in reference to the most powerful myth of maternity in the West, the Virgin and child, a myth with pagan roots that replaced earlier metaphors of the female body as the spontaneously regenerating earth. The image of virgin mother and holy child that dominates religious iconography is alluded to in the opening scene of *The Scarlet Letter*. At one stroke Hawthorne overlays the Christian myth on its pagan antecedents and supplants Catholic belief with Puritan revisions and purification of Papist excess. A Papist, we are told, might see in the spectacle of Hester and her baby on the scaffold "the image of Divine Maternity" (p. 60). Hester's baby has not yet been assigned gender by the text, but the infant that the Madonna cradles is a male, the son of God.

There is more than mere irony at work in this textual reference to Mary and Jesus, to the circumstances of Immaculate Conception through the Word of the Holy Ghost. All that the child represents in the images of Divine Maternity depends on an invisible, spiritual relationship to God, mankind's origin and final end. The image of maternity that dominates our religious-cultural history is this image of mother and son, repeated in the Pietà. The spiritual transference of power takes place across Mary's body; she is the mat(t)er through which the spirit of God passes into humankind. God's word is the agent of the Immaculate Conception, and, as Julia Kristeva argues, this method of impregnation escapes not only the biological, human condition that Christ must transcend but also avoids the inevitable equation of sex with death (Kristeva 103). Hester and her baby represent a corrupted version of the Virgin Mary-Holy Child icon, of course, but the differences between these sacred and profane visions of motherhood are drawn textually through similar images. The Virgin's halo signifies her special place among women ("alone of all her sex"), while Hester's beauty "made a halo of the misfortune and ignominy in which she was enveloped" (p. 58). Commenting on Hester, a Puritan "goodwife" declares, "This woman has brought shame upon us all, and ought to die" (p.

56). Dressed in blue and white, the Virgin displays the colors of holiness and purity, while Hester is draped in somber gray, appropriate to her status as sinner. Kristeva comments that representations of the virginal body reduce female sexuality to "a mere implication," exposing only "the ear, the tears, and the breasts" (108). Hester reveals even less of herself, her entire body shrouded in gray, her hair covered by a tight-fitting cap, her breasts shielded by the scarlet letter. Hester Prynne stands before the crowd not "fully revealed" (p. 57) as the text claims, but fully concealed, her sexual body hidden by the cultural text that inscribes her. Only when she unclasps the scarlet letter from her bosom and removes the cap that confines her hair is the sexual power of her body revealed synecdochically—that is, by mere implication.

These images of maternity inscribe sexual difference around the veiled figure of the mother's body. Daughters read the mother's body as sexual text differently than do sons. Sons, including the Son of God, pass by way of the mother's body into the world of the fathers, whose work they carry on in culture and society. For the son, the mother's body inscribes the myth of sexual difference and the space of an originary otherness: it textualizes alienation and desire. For the daughter, however, the mother's body emblematizes her biological-cultural fate, her place in the reproductive chain. The female body is also the locus of patriarchal fears and sexual longing, its fertile dark continent bound and cloaked. It is a space of shame, of castration. For the daughter, the maternal body maps both her past and future; it is a space of repetition.

Pearl enters this space, however, only to escape seemingly unscathed her own fate as the living emblem of sinful, shameful passion. She slips through the umbilical knot that ties representation to repetition. Made heir to Chillingworth's wealth, she comes to stand in the place of the son, one paternal figure standing in for another, the absent (and unacknowledged) father. The sign of Pearl's altered status is her material wealth, which rewrites the maternal script: she grows up to become "the richest heiress of her day" (pp. 199–200), a circumstance that brings about "a very material change in the public estimation" of her. Material riches controvert notions of Pearl as an "elf-child" or "demon offspring" and open the possibility of her full participation in Puritan life: "had the mother and child remained here, little Pearl, at a marriageable period of life, might have mingled her wild blood with the lineage of the devoutest Puritan among them all" (p. 200). Pearl's future and final end remain matters of speculation among Salem gossips, however. Pearl leaves the Puritan community, and her mother—who returns in old age, still wearing the scarlet letter—remains silent about the circumstances of her daughter's life.

Brook Thomas on Mr. Prynne

Hawthorne may elicit our sympathy for Hester and Dimmesdale while condemning their adultery, but he generates little sympathy for Hester's husband. From Chaucer's January to various figures in Shakespeare to Charles Bovary to Leopold Bloom, the cuckolded husband has been treated with varying amounts of humor, pathos, sympathy, and contempt. Few, however, are as villainous as Roger Chillingworth. Hawthorne's treatment of him starkly contrasts with the sympathetic treatment some courts gave to cuckolded husbands in the 1840s, when various states began applying the so-called unwritten law by which a husband who killed his wife's lover in the act of adultery was acquitted. Arguments for those acquittals portrayed avenging husbands as "involuntary agents of God." In contrast, lovers were condemned as "children of Satan," "serpents," and "noxious reptiles" with supernatural power allowing them to invade the "paradise of blissful marriages" (Ireland, "Libertine" 32).[15]

In *The Scarlet Letter* this imagery is reversed. It is the avenging husband who stalks his wife's lover with "other senses than [those ministers and magistrates] possess" and who is associated with "Satan himself, or Satan's emissary" (p. 108). In the meantime, we imagine Arthur, Hester, and Pearl as a possible family (Herbert 201). The narrator so writes off Chillingworth as Hester's legal husband that he refers to him as her "former husband" (p. 136), causing Michael T. Gilmore to follow suit (93) and D. H. Lawrence to designate Mr. Prynne Hester's "first" husband. A legal scholar writing on adultery goes so far as to call Hester an "unwed mother" (Weinstein 225).

By reversing the sympathy that courts gave to cuckolded husbands taking revenge into their own hands, Hawthorne draws attention to the importance of seeking justice within the confines of the written law. Dramatizing the dangers of achieving justice outside the law, Chillingworth illustrates natural liberty's potential for evil as well as for good. On the one hand, it prompts Hester to question the law in the name of a more equitable social order. On the other, it can allow Chillingworth to take the law into his own hands for personal revenge. If Hester's desire to create the world "anew" suggests utopian possibilities, Chillingworth's revenge, driven by "new interests" and "a new purpose" (p. 102), suggests the potential for a reign of terror. Hawthorne links these two seeming opposites through the secret pact that Hester and her husband forge on his return. Their secret bond in turn parallels the secret bond of natural lovers that Hester and Dimmesdale contemplate in their meeting in the forest. The two bonds even have structural similarities. For instance, just as Hester's new bond with her husband can be maintained only because he has taken on a new name, so Hester counsels her lover, "Give up this name of Arthur Dimmesdale, and make thyself another" (p. 157). More importantly, the secrecy in which both bonds are made isolates everyone involved from the human community. As such, both are in stark contrast to the bond created by the civil ceremony of marriage whose public witness links husband and wife to the community.

Much has been made of Hester's adulterous violation of her marriage vows. Not much attention, however, has been paid to her husband's violation of his vows, even though the narrator comments on it. For instance, in prison Hester asks her husband why he will "not announce thyself openly, and cast me off at once?" His reply: "It may be . . . because I will not encounter the dishonor that besmirches the husband of a faithless woman. It may be for other reasons. Enough, it is to my purpose to live and die unknown" (p. 73). In legal terms, Chillingworth's fear of dishonor makes no sense inasmuch as he has committed no crime. But if some antebellum courts displayed great sympathy to cuckolded husbands through the unwritten law, there was a long tradition—still powerful in the seventeenth century—of popular and bawdy rituals mocking cuckolded husbands (Ramsey 202–07). No matter what other motives Chillingworth might have, the narrator makes clear that the man "whose connection with the fallen woman had been the most intimate and sacred of them all" resolves "not to be pilloried beside her on her pedestal of shame" (p. 101). That resolve explains "why—since the choice was with himself—" he does not "come forward to vindicate his claim to an inheritance so little desirable" (p. 101).

According to coverture, that undesirable inheritance was not only Hester, but also her child. Fully aware of his husbandly rights, Chillingworth tells his wife, "Thou and thine, Hester Prynne, belong to me" (p. 73). Nonetheless, he refuses to acknowledge his inheritance, telling Hester in the same scene, "The child is yours,—she is none of mine,—neither will she recognize my voice or aspect as a father's" (p. 70). The doctrine of coverture was clearly a patriarchal institution; nonetheless, it was not solely to the advantage of the husband. It was also a means to hold him responsible for the well-being of his wife and children. Chillingworth might not be Pearl's biological father, but he was her father in the eyes of the law. That legal status adds another dimension to the recognition scene that occurs when Chillingworth walks out of the forest and finds his wife on public display for having committed adultery. "Speak, woman!" he "coldly and sternly" cries from the crowd. "Speak; and give your child a father!" (p. 68). Commanding his wife to reveal the name of her lover, the wronged husband also inadvertently reminds us that at any moment Hester could have given Pearl a legal father by identifying him. Even more important, Chillingworth could have identified himself. But the same man who knows his legal rights of possession as a husband refuses to take on his legal responsibilities as a father.

Pearl, in other words, has not one but two fathers who refuse to accept their responsibilities. Having lost his own father as a young boy and doubting his ability financially to support his children on losing his job at the Custom House, Hawthorne was acutely aware of the need for fathers to live up to their name. In fact, by the end of the novel he ensures Pearl's future by having her two fathers finally accept their responsibilities. At his death Dimmesdale publicly acknowledges his paternity, eliciting from Pearl a "pledge that she would grow up amid human joy and sorrow, nor for ever do battle with the world" (p. 197). At his death Chillingworth bequeaths to his once-rejected inheritance "a very considerable amount of property, both here and in England" (p. 199). Even so, the book's emphasis on failed fathers raises the possibility that Hester will earn her claim to good citizenship through her role as a mother.

Note

15. For more on cases involving the "unwritten law," see Ireland, "Insanity"; Hartog; and Ganz.

LAURA DOYLE EXPLORES
HAWTHORNE'S TWO HISTORIES

In *The Scarlet Letter*, colonization just happens or, more accurately, has just happened. We might recall, by contrast, how Catharine Maria Sedgwick's novel *Hope Leslie* elaborately narrates the sociopolitical process of making an Indian village into a native English spot. Hawthorne eclipses this drama of settlement. Although Hawthorne, like Sedgwick, sets his plot of sexual crisis in the early colonial period of Stuart political crisis and English Civil War, he places these events in the distant backdrop, as remote from his seventeenth-century characters as his nineteenth-century readers. . . .

In beginning from this already fallen moment, Hawthorne keeps off-stage both the "fall" of colonization and its sexual accompaniment. He thereby obscures his relationship to a long Atlantic literary and political history. But if we attend to the colonizing processes submerged in *The Scarlet Letter*, we discover the novel's place in transatlantic history—a history catalyzed by the English Civil War and imbued with that conflict's rhetoric of native liberty. We see that Hawthorne's text partakes of an implicitly racialized, Atlantic ur-narrative, in which a people's quest for freedom entails an ocean crossing and a crisis of bodily ruin. . . .

Criticism on *The Scarlet Letter* makes clear that the novel is a historical palimpsest—with a surface as illegible and in need of translation as the archaic, "gules" *A*. Not just one but two histories are submerged here, one contemporary with Hester and one with Hawthorne. Or rather, as I will argue, what is ultimately submerged is the deep connection between these two histories—that is, the uninterrupted project of colonization.

Many earlier critics of the novel consider it both a critique and an expression of American Puritanism, and most of these critics share Hawthorne's sense of that legacy as *the* cultural origin of U.S. national history. In his 1880 book, *Hawthorne*, Henry James helped to establish the identification between Hawthorne and the Puritan tradition, invoking the notion of a racial inheritance when he concludes that *The Scarlet Letter* is utterly "impregnated with that after-sense of the old Puritan consciousness of life" and that indeed the "qualities of his ancestors filtered down through generations into his composition," so that "*The Scarlet Letter* was, as it were, the vessel that gathered up the last of the precious drops."[24] . . . Building on the notion that Hawthorne's very dissent made him the child of Puritan America, early-twentieth-century scholars tracked Hawthorne's knowledge of Puritan sources and studied his main characters as they suffer under and, perhaps, redeem that legacy.

More recently, however, an increasing number of scholars place the novel explicitly within the political concerns of the volatile 1840s. These critics call attention to the fact that in the decade leading up to Hawthorne's writing of *The Scarlet Letter*, the nation was embroiled in conflict over a range of issues—the Indian Removal Acts, the annexation of western territories and war with Mexico, the Fugitive Slave Law, the 1848 Women's Convention in Seneca Falls, and the spectre (as many felt it) of the European revolutions of 1848. Accordingly, they have considered the novel's drama of law, punishment, dissent, and consent as a coded exploration of a citizen's proper response to these matters. In many of these readings, Hawthorne's vanishing allusions to Indians, his absence of allusions to slavery, and his conservative closure with Hester's final return appear as evidence of his investment in what Sacvan Bercovitch deems a liberal process of compromise and consensus, which ultimately advises that obedience to the law, however flawed the law may be (even if it meant sending escaped African Americans back into slavery), ultimately sets the nation free.[27] Others, however, have highlighted the same ambiguity earlier critics celebrated, finding in the narrator's sinuous movements and undecidable equivocations an invitation to readers to become active interpreters and, by extension, sympathetic, questioning citizens, including of the law.[28] . . .

It seems clear to me that in *The Scarlet Letter* at least, Hawthorne stills the volatility and veils the violence of the Massachusetts Puritan community for his readers, even as he may coyly signal their suppressed presence. . . . For operating hand in hand with his muffling of political instability in Massachusetts are his suppressions of this colony's involvement not only in Indian wars but also in a transatlantic political crisis that would culminate with a king's beheading in 1649—the very year that Hester and Dimmesdale's relationship comes to its final crisis and Hawthorne's story-proper ends.[33] In short, Hawthorne's story, as he well knows, takes place in a colony flanked on one side by the peopled and troubled nation of England and on the other side by the peopled and troubled nations of Indian America, but as I will show presently,

Hawthorne largely de-peoples these adjacent, interlocking communities. His softening of the violence (toward a woman such as Hester) within the colony extends to making absent the foundational violence of colonization.

That is, just as Hawthorne lifts the magistrates up onto a balcony and lifts Hester up onto a scaffold—neither of which is historically accurate—so he raises his history up out of the mess of Atlantic maneuvering in 1642—and, by extension, also keeps it at one remove from what Bercovitch characterizes as the "deep cultural anxiety" circulating in the 1840s.[34]

Notes

24. Henry James, *Hawthorne* (New York: Harper and Brothers, 1880), quoted in The Critical Response to Nathaniel Hawthorne's "The Scarlet Letter," ed. Gary Scharnhorst (New York: Greenwood, 1992), 79. See also Scharnhorst's discussion of James's biography in his introduction (xvii–xix).

27. For Sacvan Berkovitch's argument, see his *The Office of the Scarlet Letter* (Baltimore: Johns Hopkins Univ. Press, 1991). Most readings acknowledge the ambiguity of voice and position in Hawthorne's work, but for critics who, like Berkovitch, align him most fully with a traditionalist orientation, see, for instance, David Leverenz, "Mrs. Hawthorne's Headache," *Nineteenth-Century Fiction* 37 (March 1983): 552–75; Myra Jehlen, "The Novel and the Middle Class in America," in *Ideology and Classic American Literature*, ed. Sacvan Bercovitch and Myra Jehlen (Cambridge, Eng.: Cambridge Univ. Press, 1986), 125–144; Jennifer Fleischner, "Hawthorne and the Politics of Slavery," *Studies in the Novel* 23 (spring 1990): 514–33; Larry J. Reynolds, *European Revolutions and the American Literary Renaissance* (New Haven: Yale Univ. Press, 1988), 79–96; Deborah Madsen, "'A' for Abolition: Hawthorne's Bond-Servant and the Shadow of Slavery," *Journal of American Studies* 25 (August 1991): 255–59; Gillian Brown, "Hawthorne, Inheritance, and Women's Property," *Studies in the Novel* 23 (spring 1991): 107–18; Deborah Gussman, "Inalienable Rights: Fictions of Political Identity in Hobomok and The Scarlet Letter," *College Literature* 22 (June 1995): 58–80; Lucy Maddox, *Removals: Nineteenth-Century American Literature and the Politics of Indian Affairs* (New York: Oxford Univ. Press, 1991); Laura Hanft Korobkin, "The Scarlet Letter of the Law: Hawthorne and Criminal Justice," *NOVEL: A Forum on Fiction* 30 (winter 1997): 193–217; and Renée Bergland, *The National Uncanny: Indian Ghosts and American Subjects* (Hanover, N.H.: University Press of New England, 2000); further references

to The National Uncanny will be cited parenthetically as NU. See also Jamie Barlowe's study of the ways Hawthorne criticism has perpetuated this conservatism in overlooking the work of women scholars on Hawthorne (*The Scarlet Mob of Scribblers* [Carbondale: Southern Illinois Univ. Press, 2000]).

28. Critics who acknowledge Hawthorne's conservative gestures of containment but nonetheless consider his ambiguous narrative voice or his romance form an expression of subversive impulses include Michael Bell, *Hawthorne and the Historical Romance of New England* (Princeton, N.J.: Princeton Univ. Press, 1971); Evan Carton, *The Rhetoric of American Romance: Dialectic and Identity in Emerson, Dickinson, Poe, and Hawthorne* (Baltimore: Johns Hopkins Univ. Press, 1985); Gordon Hutner, *Secrets and Sympathy: Forms of Disclosure in Hawthorne's Novels* (Athens: Univ. of Georgia Press, 1988); Robert S. Levine, *Conspiracy and Romance: Studies in Brockden Brown, Cooper, Hawthorne, and Melville* (New York: Cambridge Univ. Press, 1989); Lauren Berlant, *The Anatomy of National Fantasy: Hawthorne, Utopia, and Everyday Life* (Chicago: Univ. of Chicago Press, 1991), although Berlant seems to give equal emphasis to Hawthorne's double impulses to subvert and conserve; Richard Millington, *Practicing Romance: Narrative Form and Cultural Engagement in Hawthorne's Fiction* (Princeton, N.J.: Princeton Univ. Press, 1992); Emily Budick, *Engendering Romance: Women Writers and the Hawthorne Tradition, 1850–1990* (New Haven: Yale Univ. Press, 1994); Brook Thomas, "Citizen Hester: *The Scarlet Letter* as Civic Myth," *American Literary History* 13 (summer 2001): 181–211; and Peter J. Bellis, *Writing Revolution: Aesthetics and Politics in Hawthorne, Whitman, and Thoreau* (Athens: Univ. of Georgia Press, 2003).

33. The novel opens in June of 1642, and it is "seven long years" later, in 1649 (as Hawthorne mentions more than once), that Dimmesdale gives his Election Day sermon (101, 153).

34. Bercovitch, *The Office of the Scarlet Letter*, 152.

JANE F. THRAILKILL ON THE DOCTOR AND THE MINISTER

Henry James, in his early evaluation of *The Scarlet Letter*, astutely noted that the novel's dramatic center lay not with the chastened Hester Prynne—who "becomes, really, after the first scene, an accessory figure"—but with the two men who had shared her bed: "The story," James observed, "goes on for the most part between the lover and the husband." James's emphasis on the intensity of the men's bond, and his description of the doubleness of Roger Chillingworth's attentiveness to Arthur Dimmesdale, calls attention to the novelty of Hawthorne's portrayal, in which Chillingworth appears (in James's words) "to minister to his [Dimmesdale's] hidden ailment and to sympathise with his pain" while "revel[ing] in his unsuspected knowledge of these things and stimulat[ing] them by malignant arts."1 The ersatz physician does not merely attend to his patient's symptoms but also reads them, testing and modulating his evolving interpretation of their significance by eliciting from the preacher telltale spasms and winces. Dimmesdale, in short, offers up to his observant companion a literal body of evidence, a set of physiological and affective traces of actions past. . . .

Throughout his fiction, Hawthorne critiques a ponderous materialism that would reduce the world to matter emptied of spiritual purpose or higher meaning, and to a large extent he equates this position with men of science and medicine.[21] . . . Writing in *The Scarlet Letter* of the relative absence of doctors in the Puritan community, Hawthorne speculates, "In their researches into the human frame, it may be that the higher and more subtile faculties of such men were materialized, and that they lost the spiritual view of existence amid the intricacies of that wondrous mechanism, which seemed to involve art enough to comprise all of life within itself" (88). . . .

Hawthorne's interest in the townspeople's reaction to Chillingworth, then, is crucially epistemological. Even milder versions of the Bostonians' faith-based reasoning, which take vivid form in the image of Chillingworth flying through the air, understand the physician's arrival in religious terms: "Individuals of wiser faith, indeed, who knew that Heaven promotes its purposes without aiming at the stage-effect of what is called miraculous interposition, were inclined to see a providential hand in Roger Chillingworth's so opportune arrival" (90). As the historical example of Jonathan Edwards would indicate, with his empirical investigations into natural phenomena and experimentation with the smallpox vaccine, the power of the divine account of natural occurrences is made manifest in its capacity both to account for physical phenomena and unproblematically to digest alternate theories that, from the perspective of later observers such as Hawthorne, would come to seem at mortal odds with a divine or supernatural interpretation.[25] And just as, for the devout Puritan, there was no element of human experience that was too vulgar or terrestrial (an infected eye, say) to be assimilated to the spiritual point of view, so for a medical practitioner during Hawthorne's time there was no element of human life that was too incorporeal or intangible (a vague dread, say) to be laden with physiological significance.

But whereas his colleagues see no problem or danger in assimilating the material to the spiritual, and indeed do so reflexively, it is Dimmesdale himself who sets the material and the spiritual at odds when he asserts that the two realms are utterly divergent. Ironically, then, it is the young minister and not the aging scholar who makes the initial appeal to dualism, a conception at the philosophical heart of scientific medicine. This dualism holds that the material of the world has an existence separable from the apprehension of it by consciousness, a philosophical stance that engenders the scientific value of objectivity, in which things in the world are known in and of themselves without the adulterations of human interests and values. Having experienced the danger of mixing the carnal and the spiritual in his relationship with Hester, the transformed and guilt-ridden Dimmesdale brings added force and rigidity to his belief in their separation. This dualistic commitment subtends the minister's protest that he needs no treatment by a doctor; in this he indicates that his complaint, linked to sin and therefore spiritual at base, has a source and a cure that was outside of the realm of organic illness. Dimmesdale in fact understands his illness as a means or instrument by which the spiritual might divest itself of the material once and for all: "'I could be well content, that my labors, and my sorrows, and my sins, and my pains, should shortly end with me, and what is earthly of them be buried in my grave, and the spiritual go with me to my eternal state'" (90). Death, from this perspective, is the ultimate distillery, extracting the valuable spiritual essence from the mere clay of the body.[26] Members of Dimmesdale's congregation "best acquainted with his habits" (89) understand his dwindling physical presence in precisely these spiritualized terms when they attribute his decline to "the fasts and vigils of which he made a frequent practice, in order to keep the grossness of this earthly state from clogging and obscuring his spiritual lamp" (89).

Dimmesdale's fellow clerics, however, counter this equation, in which a decrease in physical force indicates a commensurate increase in spiritual power. They urge the young minister to accept the doctor's ministrations not merely as physical balm, but as holy "aid which Providence so manifestly held out" (90), and which it would be a sin to reject. As Oliver Wendell Holmes Sr. once remarked, "We do not deny that the God of battles decides the fate of nations; but we like to have the biggest squadrons on our side, and we are particular that our soldiers should not only say their prayers, but also keep their powder dry."[27] Clear-eyed and practical, Dimmesdale's advisors are unconcerned that the drama of Providence must play itself out on the stage of the material world.

Chillingworth, in contrast to Dimmesdale, adopts the secular outlook of traditional therapeutics, which drew no firm line between the corporeal substance of a patient and the intangibles of thought and experience that impinged upon the body.[28] To early nineteenth-century practitioners, sickness constituted a sort of biographical fingerprint, and Chillingworth, accordingly, "deemed it essential, it would seem, to know the man, before attempting to do him good" (92). The scientific medicine preeminent for the second half of the nineteenth century would assert that such "soft" knowledge of a patient bore no relevance to the progress, diagnosis, or treatment of diseases understood to be specific invading entities.[29] But under the rubric of traditional therapeutics that informs *The Scarlet Letter*, no element of a person's life, character, spiritual state, or physical constitution is deemed irrelevant to his overall health and well-being. Chillingworth—and for that matter Hawthorne—wishes to cast Dimmesdale as such a patient par excellence: "Wherever there is a heart and an intellect, the diseases of the physical frame are tinged with the peculiarities of these. In Arthur Dimmesdale, thought and imagination were so active, and sensibility so intense, that the bodily infirmity would be likely to have its groundwork there" (92). The close proximity of Hester's husband to the minister is in fact the fantasy of traditional therapeutics: that a doctor might be able to harvest with an expert eye every detail of a patient's life, so that the nature of the affliction and the appropriate course of treatment would emerge from the welter of biographical detail. This impulse underlies Chillingworth's commitment to "bring[ing] his mind into such affinity with his patient's, that this last shall unawares have spoken what he imagines himself only to have thought" (92). Distinctions, or in fact discrepancies, that are important to the minister—between his secret thoughts and his public voice, between physical complaint and spiritual health, and even between himself and his physician—are confounded by the forceful presence of his assiduous attendant, who combines the epistemological modes of intuition and empiricism.

Chillingworth is therefore the force of mixing in the life of Dimmesdale, who "[i]n no state of society would . . . have been what is called a man of liberal views; it would always be essential to his peace to feel the pressure of a faith about him, supporting, while it confined him within its iron framework" (91). Erudite on a wide range of topics rather than confined to those theological, cosmopolitan in thought and action where Dimmesdale's colleagues are provincial, Chillingworth not only seeks to understand how the minister sees the world, but also to offer his patient a glimpse of his own experimental epistemology. So while much has been made of the ersatz physician's prying into the minister's life, it has been less noted that his intimacy with Dimmesdale also provides "the occasional relief of looking at the universe through the medium of another kind of intellect" (91). Again, Hawthorne links this multiplicity of perspective with romance and with nature when he writes of the two men's "long walks on the seashore, or in the forest; mingling various talk with the plash and murmur of the waves, and the solemn wind-anthem among the tree-tops" (91). The natural environment, the free-form discussions, the variety of topics—all provide a contrast with the iron theology and social forms of Puritanism. The older man draws the young minister out in talk, and in turn Dimmesdale reveals different facets of his character "when thrown amidst other moral scenery" (92) such as might be found in his home or in the forest rather than in the confining walls of the meeting house.

These wanderings are cast as both spatial and intellectual, with the presence of Chillingworth eliciting new thoughts "as if a window were thrown open, admitting a freer atmosphere into the close and stifled study, where his life was wasting itself away" (91). For while Dimmesdale inters himself in books of "monkish erudition" (93) in order to escape the world, his companion either wanders the woods looking for potent herbs or retires to "his study and laboratory . . . provided with a distilling apparatus, and the means of compounding drugs and chemicals" (93). Chillingworth exploits the investigative opportunities provided by close proximity to see how Dimmesdale reacts to a variety of different stimuli, and the young minister in turn is drawn to the older man's cosmopolitanism and experimentalism: "these two learned persons sat themselves down, each in his own domain, yet familiarly passing from one apartment to the other, and bestowing a mutual and not incurious inspection into one another's business" (93–94). This image of transit— of "familiarly passing from one apartment to the other"— encompasses the relationship of the two men, both of whom experiment with inhabiting the perspective of the other.

Notes

1. Henry James, "Nathaniel Hawthorne," in *Literary Criticism*, ed. Leon Edel (New York: Library of America, 1984), 404.

21. Taylor Stoehr, *Hawthorne's Mad Scientists: Pseudoscience and Social Science in Nineteenth-Century Life and Letters* (Hamden, CT: Archon Books, 1978), 9.

25. In Jonathan Edwards, Perry Miller writes, "He is the last great American, perhaps the last European, for whom there could be no warfare between religion and science, or between ethics and nature.

He was incapable of accepting Christianity and physics on separate premises" (New York: William Sloane Associates, 1949), 72.

26. In this, Dimmesdale participates in an activity that, according to Sharon Cameron, is central to Hawthorne's short-story characters who "try to create a division between their own corporeal essence and the meaning of that corporeality." *The Corporeal Self: Allegories of the Body in Melville and Hawthorne* (New York: Columbia Univ. Press, 1981), 79.

27. Oliver Wendell Holmes, "The Contagiousness of Puerperal Fever," in *Medical Essays*, Vol. 9 of *The Works of Oliver Wendell Holmes*, 13 vols. (Boston: Houghton Mifflin and Co., 1892), 125.

28. The profound interpenetration of states of mind and states of body in nineteenth-century medicine should not be confused with modern medicine's willingness to label certain illnesses "psychosomatic." Such a term only becomes operative once the categories of physiology and psychology have become firmly established, in order to distinguish those "unusual" instances of border crossing. In traditional therapeutics, no such term was necessary.

29. Historian of science Owsei Temkin has written of the similarities between modern theories of disease entities and ancient religious ideas about demonic possession. See "An Historical Analysis of the Concept of Infection" in *The Double Face of Janus* (Baltimore: Johns Hopkins Univ. Press, 1977), 457–71.

GALE TEMPLE ADDRESSES MASCULINE AMBIVALENCE IN *THE SCARLET LETTER*

Near the end of *The Scarlet Letter*, Dimmesdale is faced with a choice. He can either make good on the plan he has made with Hester to form a "proper" family in a distant land, or he can remain in Puritan Boston, write and deliver his election-day sermon, and confess publicly his involvement with Hester and Pearl. He chooses the latter, of course, and in so doing becomes a martyr for the well-being of the status quo.[9] His subject matter, which creates in his auditors uproarious excitement and admiration ("never had man spoken in so wise, so high, and so holy a spirit, as he that spake this day"), is rather vague, in the narrator's account but it concerns the "high and glorious destiny for the newly gathered people of the Lord" in New England—a nonspecific yet wholly affirmative message (*CE*, 1:249). It is appropriate that Dimmesdale should deliver such a sermon in the marketplace, for his election-day speech symbolizes a particularly saleable ideal, one that renounces self-doubt, internal angst, and shame over historical precedent (both individual and collective) and urges citizen-consumers to forge ahead with hope and innocence into the always promising future.[10]

As several recent critical takes on the novel have suggested, Dimmesdale's choice is consistent with his panicked flight from the probing intimacy of Roger Chillingworth, who makes it his life's work to "[dig] into the poor clergyman's heart, like a miner searching for gold" (*CE*, 1:129). Scott Derrick argues that the "central effort" of Hawthorne's novel is "the homophobic control of the disruptive eroticism of Dimmesdale's relation to Chillingworth," whom Derrick views as a sort of "(pre)homosexual."[11] Lora Romero similarly argues that the Dimmesdale/Chillingworth subplot indexes "the structural conditions of male–male relationships in the homophobic culture which we share with Hawthorne."[12] By fleeing the threat of Chillingworth's altogether too ardent interest in his own mind and body, delivering an inspiring speech about the glorious hope and promise of America's future, and then publicly announcing an obviously heterosexual, albeit unsanctioned, "sin" with Hester, Dimmesdale secures for himself what he feels is a safer, more socially acceptable identity form.[13]

Dimmesdale's decision is a predictable one given Hawthorne's conceptualization of the civic sphere, which is predicated on citizens tacitly acknowledging various forms of illicit desire in themselves and others but leaving the throbbing actualities of sin tactfully where they belong—closeted away in the private home or in the dark recesses of the psychic interior. Dimmesdale's popularity as a minister is a case in point, for it owes less to his superior piety than to his particular talent for revealing just enough inner suffering to create sympathetic bonds with other community members.

Dimmesdale's flight from Chillingworth situates the young cleric firmly within a sanctioned space of ostensibly normal, albeit withered, masculine desire. And significantly,

Dimmesdale's decision to renounce Chillingworth links him with what might be considered a more market-friendly philosophical worldview, for his election-day speech is consistent with the rhetoric of hope, optimism, and civic reformation that has defined characterizations of the "New World" since the time of the Puritans. What is more, Dimmesdale's message is reminiscent in a general way of the self-affirming plots of the popular fiction that saturated the literary marketplace in Hawthorne's day. From the perspective of the novel, then, "normal," domestically oriented, heterosexual bonds are inextricably linked with normative forms of writing and oratory.

Chillingworth, conversely, represents a far darker and more disturbing view of the writer figure, a type that recurs throughout Hawthorne's fiction. He is the character who goes altogether too far in unearthing and uprooting the secrets of nature and of the private demons that invest and constitute the stuff of subjectivity for Hawthorne. Ethan Brand, Aylmer, Rappaccini, Westervelt and Coverdale, Holgrave, and Chillingworth, to name a few, all symbolize one vision of the task of the writer, which is to probe subtly beneath the surfaces and illusions of the social contract in order to dredge up and expose to light something more profound and even troubling about the human psyche. Rather than embrace the philosophical inquisitiveness and psychic/metaphysical probings embodied by the Chillingworth within, Dimmesdale chooses to exorcise this anti-systemic element of himself, purging the Roger in his soul so that he can disseminate a message of hope and self-affirmation for the always deferred future of America.

In the ambivalent, conflict-ridden bond between Chillingworth and Dimmesdale, we can see at work a struggle that is particularly significant and meaningful for Hawthorne at this time: the conflict between a desire to make money through his writing, and as such to become a proper middle-class masculine subject, and an opposing desire to write meaningful fiction that would complicate the affirmational solace offered through the productions of the "scribbling women" that Hawthorne and Melville persistently vilified.[14]

Both conceptions of the role of the writer lead to psychic impasses, for to reject the imperatives of the market is to fail as a bourgeois paterfamilias and to embrace masculine economic productivity is tantamount to an agonizing and paralyzing form of self-suspension, one that negatively affects the capacity for agency and equality for both men and women.

Something similar might be said about Hawthorne's view of his relationship with Melville. Melville imagines in his 1851 letter a friendship based not on competition, power, or relative sexual and economic potency but on a sort of commingling of souls. Such a bond, Melville suggests, would render the market in many ways obsolete. He will write, he says, for Nathaniel alone. For Hawthorne, however, the very definition of heterosexual masculinity is based on proprietary self-denial and the continual deferral of all meaningful forms of consummation between men. To form an intimate bond with another man would be tantamount to rejecting a vision of himself as a marketplace-oriented provider, a man on a quest for a self-made self forever receding into the horizon. This is the dilemma, then, facing Hawthorne as he begins his relationship with Melville in the Berkshires, a friendship that would catalyze a series of artistic and personal choices in both men's lives. Hawthorne's career seems to have followed a path very similar to the one charted in *The Scarlet Letter*, for his life became increasingly more domestically mainstream, but in his art he continued to hint at the various desires and psychoses that forever shadow the body of normative ideology.

Notes

9. On Hawthorne's fiction as staging moments of capitulatory compromise, see Bercovitch, *Office of "The Scarlet Letter."*

10. The historical context for *The Scarlet Letter* is, of course, seventeenth-century Boston. As Gilmore notes, however, the plot of the novel is also fundamentally about how nineteenth-century American life was structuring itself in relation to the onset of market capitalism. See Gilmore, "Hawthorne and the Making of the Middle Class."

11. Derrick, *Monumental Anxieties*, 36.

12. Romero, *Home Fronts*, 91. See also Herbert, "Pornographic Manhood and *The Scarlet Letter*."

13. This formula of triangulated desire has famously been theorized by such gender and sexuality critics as Gail Rubin and Eve Sedgwick. See Rubin, "The Traffic in Women"; and Sedgwick, *Between Men*. For a Sedgwick/Rubin-inspired reading of *The Blithedale Romance* and *Pierre*, see Mueller, "This Infinite Fraternity of Feeling."

14. On Hawthorne's struggles with the feminized position of the writer, see Leverenz, *Manhood and the American Renaissance*; Romero, *Home Fronts*; Herbert, *Dearest Beloved*; Derrick, *Monumental Anxieties*; and Gilmore, "Hawthorne and the Making of the Middle Class."

Works by Nathaniel Hawthorne

Fanshawe: A Tale, 1828.

Twice-Told Tales, 1837.

Grandfather's Chair: A History for Youth, 1841.

Famous Old People: Being the Second Epoch of Grandfather's Chair, 1841.

Liberty Tree: With the Last Words of Grandfather's Chair, 1841.

Twice-Told Tales, expanded edition, 1842.

Biographical Stories for Children, 1842.

The Celestial Rail-Road, 1843.

Mosses from an Old Manse, 1846.

The Scarlet Letter, 1850.

The House of the Seven Gables, 1851.

A Wonder-Book for Girls and Boys, 1852.

The Snow-Image and Other Twice-Told Tales, 1852.

The Blithedale Romance, 1852.

The Life of Franklin Pierce, 1852.

Tanglewood Tales for Girls and Boys, 1853.

The Marble Faun, published first in England under the title *The Transformation*, 1860.

Our Old Home: A Series of English Sketches, 1863.

Pansie, a Fragment, 1864.

Passages from the American Note-books, edited by Sophia Peabody Hawthorne, 1868.

Passages from the English Note-Books, edited by Sophia Peabody Hawthorne, 1870.

Passages from the French and Italian Note-books, edited by Sophia Peabody Hawthorne, 1871.

Septimus, A Romance, edited by Una Hawthorne and Robert Browning, 1872.

Fanshawe and Other Pieces, 1876.

The Dolliver Romance and Other Pieces, 1876.

Dr. Grimshawe's Secret, A Romance, edited by Julian Hawthorne, 1883.

The Ghost of Doctor Harris, 1900.

Twenty Days with Julian and Little Bunny, 1904.

Annotated Bibliography

Argersinger, Jana L., and Leland S. Person, eds. *Hawthorne and Melville: Writing a Relationship*. Athens and London: The University of Georgia Press, 2008.

American writers Herman Melville and Nathaniel Hawthorne have generated volumes of critical commentary on their lives and works. Since there is much overlap in themes and backgrounds between them, they have often been compared and contrasted. Their actual friendship, however, covered only a brief period, beginning in 1850 and extending for 16 months. The editors of this recent volume make use of innovative methods for critical analysis to provide a more in-depth look at the relationship.

Barlowe, Jamie. *The Scarlet Mob of Scribblers: Rereading Hester Prynne*. Carbondale and Edwardsville: Southern Illinois University Press, 2000.

Barlowe comes to this study of Hawthorne and *The Scarlet Letter* from the perspective of genre and other related cultural divisions. She notes in particular the absence of critical commentary on Hester Prynne by women scholars. One of the most interesting chapters looks at the several movie versions of the novel, including the most recent with actress Demi Moore.

Bosco, Ronald A., and Jillmarie Murphy, eds. *Hawthorne in His Own Time*. Iowa City: University of Iowa Press, 2007.

This study of Nathaniel Hawthorne looks to the writer's contemporaries for insights about his life and writings. Using material from diaries, memoirs, letters, and interviews, the editors provide a multifaceted perspective on Hawthorne's personal and public life. Commentary by family members, childhood friends, and fellow writers such as Ralph Waldo Emerson, Henry James, and Oliver Wendell Holmes are included.

Carnes, Mark C., ed. *Novel History: Historians and Novelists Confront America's Past (and Each Other)*. New York and London: Simon & Schuster, 2001.

This volume addresses the way history is transmitted in novels, films, and textbooks. Carnes's areas of focus include: religion and culture (in which his discussion of *The Scarlet Letter* appears); the West as region and idea; slavery; and war.

Crain, Patricia. *The Story of A: The Alphabetization of America from "The New England Primer" to "The Scarlet Letter"*. Stanford, California: Stanford University Press, 2000.

Anyone who has heard the phrase—"As easy as ABC"—will be interested in the research and speculation presented in this study of language and literacy. The author examines learning modes in the American colonial period and traces the transformation in the way knowledge is organized and transmitted in American history through the first half of the nineteenth century. Crain uses *The Scarlet Letter* as an example of a specific understanding of letters and language: "What are the conditions of possibility for a novel whose central character is the first letter of the alphabet?" (Prologue 11)

Kopley, Richard. *The Threads of "The Scarlet Letter": A Study of Hawthorne's Transformative Art*. Newark: University of Delaware Press and London: Associated University Presses, 2003.

This work of literary history traces the influences on and of Nathaniel Hawthorne's most frequently read novel. The author traces these influences in the writings of Edgar Allan Poe, James Russell Lowell, and Ebenezer Wheelwright. An extensive bibliography is included.

Levin, Harry. *The Power of Blackness: Hawthorne, Poe, Melville*. New York: Vintage Books, 1960.

Although its main focus is the work of three American writers, Levin's study looks at a century of American writing to illuminate the darker side of the American Dream.

Murfin, Ross C., ed. *Nathaniel Hawthorne: "The Scarlet Letter."* Boston and New York: Bedford/St. Martin's Press, 2006.

This volume from the Case Studies in Contemporary Criticism series provides a comprehensive look at *The Scarlet Letter*. It offers a section on the historical and cultural context for the novel along with reviews it received on publication. A second section includes contemporary criticism using recent innovative methods of literary analysis. The volume concludes with a glossary of terms relevant to *The Scarlet Letter*, in particular, and to contemporary literary criticism in general

Reid, Margaret. *Cultural Secrets as Narrative Form: Storytelling in Nineteenth-Century America*. Columbus: The Ohio State University Press, 2004.

In this study the author looks at three seminal works of American fiction—James Fenimore Cooper's *The Spy*, Nathaniel Hawthorne's *The Scarlet Letter*, and Owen Wister's *The Virginian*. She is interested in the way each work represents a story, the telling of which is critical for the survival of the next cultural period. "Each text . . . suggests an understanding of itself as an expression of a world at a moment of transition. These are cultural moments imagined and predicted to be significant not only to their contemporary audiences but also to future generations" (Introduction xii).

Contributors

Harold Bloom is Sterling Professor of the Humanities at Yale University. Educated at Cornell and Yale universities, he is the author of more than 30 books, including *Shelley's Mythmaking* (1959), *The Visionary Company* (1961), *Blake's Apocalypse* (1963), *Yeats* (1970), *The Anxiety of Influence* (1973), *A Map of Misreading* (1975), *Kabbalah and Criticism* (1975), *Agon: Toward a Theory of Revisionism* (1982), *The American Religion* (1992), *The Western Canon* (1994), *Omens of Millennium: The Gnosis of Angels, Dreams, and Resurrection* (1996), *Shakespeare: The Invention of the Human* (1998), *How to Read and Why* (2000), *Genius: A Mosaic of One Hundred Exemplary Creative Minds* (2002), *Hamlet: Poem Unlimited* (2003), *Where Shall Wisdom Be Found?* (2004), and *Jesus and Yahweh: The Names Divine* (2005). In addition, he is the author of hundreds of articles, reviews, and editorial introductions. In 1999, Professor Bloom received the American Academy of Arts and Letters' Gold Medal for Criticism. He has also received the International Prize of Catalonia, the Alfonso Reyes Prize of Mexico, and the Hans Christian Andersen Bicentennial Prize of Denmark.

Jamie Barlowe teaches English and women's studies at the University of Toledo. She has published several essays in journals and collections such as *American Literary History*; *Women and Language*; and *Common Ground: Feminist Collaboration in the Academy*.

Patricia Crain has published additional work on Hawthorne including the *Encyclopedia of American Poetry: The Nineteenth Century* (1998).

David S. Reynolds teaches in the English and American studies department at Baruch College and the Graduate Center of the City University of New York. Other published work includes: *Walt Whitman's America: A Cultural Biography* (1995), *Beneath the American Renaissance: The Subversive Imagination in the Age of*

Emerson and Melville (1989), and *Faith in Fiction: The Emergence of Religious Literature in America* (1981).

Hal Blythe and **Charlie Sweet** co-wrote and published many essays in journals such as *The Writer* (2003), *The Writer's Handbook* (2004), and *The Writer's Chronicle* (2003).

Monika M. Elbert teaches in the English department at Montclair State University where she is also the editor of *The Nathaniel Hawthorne Review*. She is the editor of *Separate Spheres No More: Gender Convergence in Nineteenth-Century American Literature 1830–1930* (2000).

Shari Benstock teaches in the English department at the University of Miami. She directs the Women's Series Program there and edits a series on feminist criticism, *Reading Women Writing*. Her other published works include: *Women of the Left Bank: Paris, 1900–1940* (1987); *Textualizing the Feminine: On the Limits of Genre* (1991); *No Gifts from Chance* (1994), a biography of Edith Wharton; and, as co-editor, *A Handbook of Literary Feminisms* (2002).

Brook Thomas teaches in the English and comparative literature department at the University of California at Irvine. His publications include: *American Literary Realism and the Failed Promise of Contract* (1997); *The New Historicism and Other Old-Fashioned Topics* (1991); and *Cross-examinations of Law and Literature: Cooper, Hawthorne, Stowe, and Melville* (1987).

Laura Doyle teaches in the English department at the University of Massachusetts at Amherst where she is also the director of the undergraduate studies in English program. In addition to her work on Hawthorne, she has published *Freedom's Empire: Race and the Rise of the Novel in Atlantic Modernity, 1640–1940*.

Jane F. Thrailkill is the author of *Affecting Fictions: Mind, Body, and Emotion in American Literary Realism* and has published essays on the intersections of literature, science, and philosophy in the journals *American Literature*, *English Literary History*, and *Studies in American Fiction*.

Gale Temple is an assistant professor in the English department at the University of Alabama at Birmingham. His most recent work is a manuscript looking at the way addiction is portrayed in early American fiction.

Acknowledgments

Jamie Barlowe, "ReReading Women: Hester-Prynne-ism." From *The Scarlet Mob of Scribblers: Rereading Hester Prynne*, pp. 14–18, 128–30. Published by Southern Illinois University Press. Copyright © 2000 by the Board of Trustees, Southern Illinois University.

Patricia Crain, "Allegory, Adultery, Alphabetization." From *The Story of A: The Alphabetization of America from* The New England Primer *to* The Scarlet Letter, pp. 191–98, 262–65. Published by Stanford University Press. Copyright © 2000 by the Board of Trustees of Leland Stanford Junior University.

David S. Reynolds, "Hawthorne's Cultural Demons: History, Popular Culture, and *The Scarlet Letter.*" From *Novel History: Historians and Novelists Confront America's Past (and Each Other)*, pp. 229–34. Published by Simon & Schuster. Copyright © 2001 by Mark C. Carnes.

Hal Blythe and Charlie Sweet, "Hawthorne's Dating Problem in *The Scarlet Letter.*" From *American Notes and Queries/ANQ* 16, no. 3 (Summer 2003): 35–37. Copyright © 2003 *ANQ*.

Monika M. Elbert, "'A' as Hester's Autonomy in Nathaniel Hawthorne's *The Scarlet Letter* (1850)." From *Women in Literature: Reading Through the Lens of Gender*, edited by Jerilyn Fisher and Ellen S. Silber, pp. 256–58. Published by Greenwood Press. Copyright © 2003 by Jerilyn Fisher and Ellen S. Silber.

Shari Benstock, "Mother as Matter." From *The Scarlet Letter. Case Studies in Contemporary Criticism*, edited by Ross C. Murfin, pp. 405–09. Copyright © 2006 by Bedford/St. Martin's.

Brook Thomas, "Another View of Mr. Prynne," From *The Scarlet Letter. Case Studies in Contemporary Criticism*, edited by

Ross C. Murfin, pp. 443–47. Copyright © 2006 by Bedford/ St. Martin's.

Laura Doyle, "'A' for Atlantic: The Colonizing Force of Hawthorne's *The Scarlet Letter*." From *American Literature* 79, no. 2 (June 2007): 250–55, 269–71. Copyright © 2007 by Duke University Press.

Jane F. Thrailkill, "*The Scarlet Letter*: Romantic Medicine." From *Studies in American Fiction* 34, no. 1 (Spring 2006): n.p. Copyright © 2006 Northeastern University.

Gale Temple, "Masculine Ambivalence in *The Scarlet Letter*." From *Hawthorne and Melville: Writing a Relationship*, edited by Jana L. Argersinger and Leland S. Person. Copyright © 2008 by the University of Georgia Press.

Every effort has been made to contact the owners of copyrighted material and secure copyright permission. Articles appearing in this volume generally appear much as they did in their original publication with few or no editorial changes. In some cases, foreign language text has been removed from the original essay. Those interested in locating the original source will find the information cited above.

Index